Know It, Show It

GRADE 3

Printed in the U.S.A.

ISBN 978-0-358-19208-4

8 9 10 11 12 13   0139   29 28 27 26 25 24 23 22

4500855361

r7.20

Grade
3

Contents

Short Vowels *a, e, i, o, u*

> Read each sentence. Identify the vowel sound in the underlined word. Below the sentence, circle the correct vowel sound.

1. Have you seen my yellow <u>hat</u>?
   short *a*   short *e*   short *i*   short *o*   short *u*

2. <u>Mom</u> went for a walk.
   short *a*   short *e*   short *i*   short *o*   short *u*

3. It is Rami's <u>job</u> to wash the dishes after dinner.
   short *a*   short *e*   short *i*   short *o*   short *u*

4. Lia will turn <u>ten</u> years old next month.
   short *a*   short *e*   short *i*   short *o*   short *u*

5. We like to play in the <u>sand</u> at the beach.
   short *a*   short *e*   short *i*   short *o*   short *u*

6. Ouch, that <u>pin</u> is sharp!
   short *a*   short *e*   short *i*   short *o*   short *u*

7. Jared <u>fed</u> the dog.
   short *a*   short *e*   short *i*   short *o*   short *u*

8. The purple <u>rug</u> felt soft under my feet.
   short *a*   short *e*   short *i*   short *o*   short *u*

9. The <u>ship</u> had many sails.
   short *a*   short *e*   short *i*   short *o*   short *u*

10. I got <u>mud</u> on my boots when I played in the rain.
    short *a*   short *e*   short *i*   short *o*   short *u*

Name _____

Critical Vocabulary

You can use the words you learn from reading as you talk and write.

▶ **Use what you learned about the Critical Vocabulary words to help you finish each sentence.**

1. My nose **scrunches** up when _____ .

2. Mom said that my sweater and pants **clash** because _____ .

3. It helps to be **bilingual** when _____ .

4. I am **winking** at my friend because _____ .

5. A friend might **suggest** a different game when _____ .

6. I knew the gloves were **mismatched** because _____ .

7. My sandwich is **mushy** because _____ .

8. If I go home the **usual** way, I know _____ .

▶ **Choose two of the Critical Vocabulary words and use them in a sentence. Include clues to each word's meaning in your sentence.**

_____

_____

Literary Elements

Literary elements are the pieces that make up a story. **Characters** are the people and animals in a story. The **setting** is where and when the story takes place. **Plot** includes the events that happen in a story.

▶ **Answer the questions about pages 18–19 of** *Marisol McDonald Doesn't Match.*

1. What might Marisol mean when she says "I don't match"? What details in the illustration help you know what she means?

_____

_____

_____

2. What do Marisol's statement that she doesn't match and her response to her cousin tell you about her character?

_____

_____

▶ **Answer the questions about page 29 of** *Marisol McDonald Doesn't Match.*

3. What makes Marisol a major character?

_____

4. Who is the minor character on this page? Why?

_____

5. How does this minor character affect the plot?

_____

_____

Name _____

Short Vowels a, e, i, o, u

▶ **Read each sentence. Read the vowel sound under the blank. Then find a word from the box that contains that vowel sound and makes sense in the sentence. Write the word in cursive in the blank.**

Short *a*	Short *e*	Short *i*	Short *o*	Short *u*
apple	pencil	instantly	otters	supper
captain	ending	important	shopping	under

1. May I borrow a _____ to write something?

short *e*

2. Be sure to study for the _____ test on Friday.

short *i*

3. Regina is _____ of the girl's soccer team.

short *a*

4. The river is home to animals such as fish, ducks, and _____ .

short *o*

5. I looked for my lost notebook and found it _____ my bed.

short *u*

6. Rico ate a shiny red _____ for a snack.

short *a*

7. The magician made a flower appear _____ before our eyes.

short *i*

8. Don't tell me the _____ of the book until I have finished reading it!

short *e*

9. When I grew out of my shoes, Dad took me _____ for new ones.

short *o*

10. We ate chicken and corn on the cob for _____ .

short *u*

Name _____

Prefixes mis- and un-

A **prefix** is a word part added to the beginning of a base word that changes the meaning of the word.

▶ **Choose a base word from the word bank and add the prefix *mis–* or *un–* to create a word that completes each sentence. Write your answer in cursive.**

broken   behaved   remembered   funny   spell

1. I dropped Mom's favorite vase, but luckily it remained _____ .

2. Tyler _____ the directions and took the wrong route.

3. When Nadya _____ in class, the teacher sent her to the principal's office.

4. If you tell a joke that is _____ , I'll laugh anyway because I'm a good friend!

5. It's easy to _____ some words, so be sure to check a dictionary.

Point of View

The narrator is the person who is telling the story. A story can be told from different **points of view** depending on who the narrator is.

- In first-person point of view, the narrator is a part of the story. This narrator uses words such as *I, me,* and *we.*

- In third-person point of view, the narrator is outside of the story. This narrator uses words such as *he, she,* and *they.*

▷ **Answer the questions about pages 18–19 of** *Marisol McDonald Doesn't Match.*

1. Who is the narrator?

_____

2. Which sentence in paragraph 1 helps you identify the narrator?

_____

3. Is this story told in first-person or third-person point of view? How can you tell?

_____

_____

Name _____

Theme

The **theme** is the moral or lesson in a piece of writing.

▶ **Answer the questions about pages 30–31 of** *Marisol McDonald Doesn't Match*.

1. What is the theme of this story?

_____

_____

2. What details throughout the plot help develop the theme?

_____

_____

_____

_____

_____

Grade 3

Module 1 • Week 1

Long Vowels a, e, i, o, u

➤ Read each clue. Write two rhyming words from the word bank to answer the clue.

base	rage	globe	joke
home	shade	skate	lime
broke	chase	plate	tone
robe	chrome	slime	phone
cage	shake	snake	trade

1. If you chase your friend around the bases on a field, you play a game of _____ _____ .

2. If a joke wasn't funny, the _____ is _____ .

3. If a lime rots, you will have _____ _____ .

4. A snake that shivers from the cold does a _____ _____ .

5. An angry bird in a cage may get _____ _____ .

6. If you put paper plates under your feet, you can go for a _____ _____ .

7. If you put on a bathrobe with a round map of the world on it, you are wearing a _____ _____ .

8. If you switch shady spots, you do a _____ _____ .

9. If you pick up a telephone, you hear a sound called a _____ _____ .

10. A shiny, silver house is a _____ _____ .

Name _____

Critical Vocabulary

You can use the words you learn from reading as you talk and write.

▷ **Read each sentence. Decide which sentence best fits the meaning of the word in bold print. Circle the letter next to that sentence.**

1. illustrate

   a. The artist added more detail to show the story's setting.

   b. The painting will hang in the museum for two weeks.

2. moody

   a. Ben's happiness suddenly changed to anger.

   b. Ben was happy all day long.

3. pesky

   a. I like a quiet spot to read, but my sister can read anywhere.

   b. I told my sister over and over not to talk to me when I read.

4. snarled

   a. The rubber bands in the bag are all the same size.

   b. The rubber bands got twisted together in the bag.

▷ **Choose two of the Critical Vocabulary words and use them in a sentence. Include clues to each word's meaning in your sentence.**

_____

_____

Name _____

Figurative Language

Figurative language helps readers imagine the author's ideas or creates a special effect.

- An **idiom** is a phrase that means something different from what its individual words literally mean.

- A **simile** compares two things using the word *like* or *as*.

- **Onomatopoeia** is a word that imitates the sound it represents.

▶ **Answer the questions about page 39 of** *Judy Moody, Mood Martian.*

1. What is the idiom in paragraph 10?

_____

2. What does the word *chill* literally mean?

_____

3. What does "chill out" mean here?

_____

4. How does the image of "Antarctica" connect to this idiom?

_____

_____

▶ **Answer the questions about page 43 of** *Judy Moody, Mood Martian.*

5. What simile does Stink use in paragraph 35?

_____

Name _____

6. Is a house literally "like a toothpick"?

_____

7. Why does the author use this simile?

_____

_____

> **Answer the questions about page 51 of *Judy Moody, Mood Martian*.**

8. Which words are examples of onomatopoeia? What senses do these words connect to?

_____

_____

Long Vowels a, e, i, o, u

▸ **Read each sentence. Find and underline the two-syllable word with a long vowel sound. Circle the long vowel sound.**

1. I ate a pancake for breakfast.
   long *a*   long *e*   long *i*   long *o*   long *u*

2. Carter likes to read alone.
   long *a*   long *e*   long *i*   long *o*   long *u*

3. Do we have spelling homework tonight?
   long *a*   long *e*   long *i*   long *o*   long *u*

4. The runners will compete for the medal.
   long *a*   long *e*   long *i*   long *o*   long *u*

5. The horse tried to escape from its pen.
   long *a*   long *e*   long *i*   long *o*   long *u*

6. Did you invite Marta to the party?
   long *a*   long *e*   long *i*   long *o*   long *u*

7. Randall had to delete the error he found as he typed.
   long *a*   long *e*   long *i*   long *o*   long *u*

8. Make sure to include everyone in the camping trip.
   long *a*   long *e*   long *i*   long *o*   long *u*

9. We had to go inside when it started to storm.
   long *a*   long *e*   long *i*   long *o*   long *u*

10. The store should reduce its prices so that they are fair.
   long *a*   long *e*   long *i*   long *o*   long *u*

Name _____

Critical Vocabulary

You can use the words you learn from reading as you talk and write.

> Use details and ideas from *Stink and the Freaky Frog Freakout* to support your answers to the questions below.

1. How often did the **Annual** Frog Neck Lake Frog Count happen?

_____

_____

2. What did Stink have to do before he **recited** frog names?

_____

_____

3. What did Stink hope would happen when he **protested** Mom's order to finish his homework?

_____

_____

> Write a sentence using two of the Critical Vocabulary words. Include clues to each word's meaning in your sentence.

_____

_____

Name _____

Literary Elements

Literary elements are the pieces that make up a story. **Characters** are the people and animals in a story. The **setting** is where and when the story takes place. **Plot** is the events that happen in a story.

▷ **Answer the questions about pages 60–61 of** *Stink and the Freaky Frog Freakout.*

1. Who is the main character?

_____

2. What challenge will Stink face in this story?

_____

_____

3. What do you learn about Stink's personality?

_____

_____

▷ **Answer the questions about pages 66–67 of** *Stink and the Freaky Frog Freakout.*

4. How does Judy help solve a problem for Stink?

_____

5. How do the text on page 66 and the illustration on page 67 show a different relationship between Stink and Judy from the one you read about in *Judy Moody, Mood Martian?*

_____

_____

Name _____

Prefix non-

A **prefix** is a word part added to the beginning of a base word that changes the meaning of the word.

▶ **Add the prefix *non–* to the words below. Then write the new word and explain each word's meaning. Then use the words to finish the story that follows.**

stop: _____ Meaning: _____

living: _____ Meaning: _____

human: _____ Meaning: _____

fiction: _____ Meaning: _____

Our teacher gave us a homework assignment. We had to write a paragraph about someone or something very different from us. We couldn't write about something make-believe, though. Our paragraph had to be

_____ .

My ideas started coming _____ , one after another.

At first, I wanted to write about something like a doorknob or a rock, because

I am alive and it is _____ . That makes it *very* different from me!

Then, I decided it would be more fun to write about an animal. An animal is

not like me because it is _____ . Which animal should I pick? I chose the octopus. I thought I didn't have much in common with an octopus, but it turns out the octopus is really smart—just like me!

Name _____

Figurative Language

Figurative language helps readers imagine the author's ideas or creates a special effect.

- A **simile** compares two things using the word *like* or *as*.

- An **idiom** is a phrase that means something different from what the words say.

- A **hyperbole** is an exaggeration.

> **Answer the questions about page 61 of *Stink and the Freaky Frog Freakout*.**

1. What is the first simile on this page? Which word signals that this is a simile?

_____

2. Is Stink really a duck? So, why does the author have Webster use this simile to describe Stink?

_____

> **Answer the questions about page 65 of *Stink and the Freaky Frog Freakout*.**

3. In paragraph 27, what is the idiom the author uses to describe the snoring sound?

_____

4. Does Stink's snoring really create a storm inside the kitchen?

_____

Name _____

5. What does the idiom mean?

_____

_____

6. How is this also an example of hyperbole?

_____

_____

Name _____

More Long a and Long e Spellings

▶ Read each sentence. Identify the vowel sound in the boldfaced word. Underline the vowel or vowel team that stands for the vowel sound in the word. Circle the name of the vowel sound below the sentence.

1. My **great** grandmother is 90 years old.

   long *a*   long *e*

2. I have to **clean** my room before I can go out.

   long *a*   long *e*

3. Let's sit in the shade of that big **tree**.

   long *a*   long *e*

4. A **thief** stole the gold coins.

   long *a*   long *e*

5. Ella chose a **plain** hot dog on a bun.

   long *a*   long *e*

6. This is the **clay** pot I formed in art class.

   long *a*   long *e*

7. Mari hoped **she** would win the prize.

   long *a*   long *e*

8. I got a letter in the **mail**!

   long *a*   long *e*

9. Can you tell me which **way** to the park?

   long *a*   long *e*

10. Goats and **sheep** live on the farm.

   long *a*   long *e*

Name _____

Critical Vocabulary

You can use the words you learn from reading as you talk and write.

▶ **Use details and ideas from *Scaredy Squirrel* to support your answers to the questions below.**

1. How does Scaredy Squirrel prepare for an **emergency**?

_____

2. What makes Scaredy Squirrel's day **predictable**?

_____

3. What **drastic** change does Scaredy Squirrel make at the end of the story?

_____

4. What does Scaredy Squirrel's first glide **distract** him from?

_____

5. What does Scaredy Squirrel learn from **venturing** out of his nut tree?

_____

6. Do you think Scaredy Squirrel will need to **consult** his Exit Plan in the future? Why or why not?

_____

_____

▶ **Choose two of the Critical Vocabulary words and use them in a sentence.**

_____

_____

Name _____

Point of View

Point of view is the answer to this question: *Who is telling the story?* It may be a narrator who is:

- part of the story. This narrator uses words such as *I, me,* and *we.*
- outside of the story. This narrator uses words such as *he, she,* and *they.*

▷ **Answer the questions about pages 76–77 of *Scaredy Squirrel.***

1. Is Scaredy Squirrel the narrator of this story? Who is the narrator?

_____

2. Is this story told in the first-person or third-person point of view? How do you know?

_____

▷ **Choose another section of *Scaredy Squirrel.***

3. What does the narrator help you to learn about Scaredy Squirrel?

_____

_____

Name _____

Suffixes –ful, –less

A **suffix** is a word part added to the end of a base word that changes the meaning of the word.

The suffix **–ful** usually changes a base word into an adjective. The suffix **–less** changes a base word into an adjective or adverb.

▷ **Add the suffix –ful or –less to the words below to form an adjective that completes each sentence. Explain the meaning of each adjective you form.**

window   cloud   wonder   end   hope   fear

1. My _____ sister will jump off even the highest diving board.

2. Mei gave a _____ performance and won first place in the competition.

3. It's a perfect day for a picnic because the sky is blue and _____ .

4. We were stuck in a _____ room, so we couldn't even look outside.

5. Bruno is _____ that his parents will let him adopt a dog.

6. The movie seemed _____ because it lasted for more than two hours.

Name _____

Text and Graphic Features

Text features include kinds of type used for emphasis, such as color, bold or italic text, and capital letters.

Graphic features, such as illustrations and diagrams, help explain ideas in the text. Illustrations show a scene from a story.

▶ **Answer the questions about pages 80–81 of *Scaredy Squirrel*.**

1. What do the two graphic lists on pages 80 and 81 compare and contrast?

_____

2. What is on each list?

_____

3. According to the lists, why might Scaredy Squirrel stay in the nut tree?

_____

4. How do the illustrations at the bottom of pages 80 and 81 help readers understand the text below the illustrations?

_____

_____

▶ **Answer the questions about page 83 of *Scaredy Squirrel*.**

5. Which words on this page stand out from the other words? How are they different from the other words?

_____

_____

6. Why did the author make these words different?

_____

_____

Name _____

More Long a and Long e Spellings

▷ Read each word in the box. Circle the letter or vowel team that stands for the long *a* or long *e* sound in each word. Some words contain both sounds. Then read each sentence. Find a word from the word bank that makes sense in the sentence. Write it in the blank.

baby	daydream
agency	apron
relaxed	creepy
seafarer	money

1. The chef wears an _____ to protect his clothes.

2. Shawna is saving her _____ for a new bike.

3. I sometimes _____ about what I will be when I grow up.

4. The old house had a dark and _____ attic.

5. My mom works at an employment _____ that helps people find work.

6. The little _____ is just two weeks old.

7. Jackson _____ in a hammock in his backyard.

8. The captain was a well-known _____ to all of the sailors on the ship.

Theme

The **theme** is the moral or lesson in a piece of writing.

> **Answer the questions about pages 92–95 of *Scaredy Squirrel*.**

1. What does Scaredy Squirrel learn about himself once he discovers he is a flying squirrel?

_____

_____

2. How does this make Scaredy Squirrel change his daily routine?

_____

_____

3. What lesson does this teach Scaredy Squirrel?

_____

_____

Name _____

More Long *o* Spellings

▶ **Read each sentence. Find the words with the long *o* sound. Then circle the vowel or vowel team that spells the sound.**

1. The captain told us the boat would float.

2. He ate a bowl of cereal and toast for breakfast.

3. She tiptoed around the lawn, looking for the toad.

4. The colt trotted across the snowy roadway.

5. Joe and Moe crowed like roosters and made Poe laugh.

▶ **Complete each sentence by filling in the blank with one long *o* word from the word bank.**

snowy	show	joke	grows

6. _____ Rose and Evie your new dress.

7. My teacher told us a funny _____ .

8. The grass _____ quickly in the summer.

9. I don't like rainy days, but I love _____ days.

Name _____

Critical Vocabulary

You can use the words you learn from reading as you talk and write.

▶ **Use details and ideas from** *Dear Primo* **to support your answers to the questions below. Write your answers in cursive. Be sure to answer in complete sentences and to leave an appropriate amount of space between words.**

1. Where does Primo Charlie like to play **video** games?

_____

_____

2. Where could you go to watch people **march**?

_____

_____

3. Why do the firefighters close off the **block** when they open a **hydrant**?

_____

_____

4. What kinds of **costumes** might you see in a parade?

_____

_____

▶ **Choose two of the Critical Vocabulary words and use them in a sentence. Include clues to each word's meaning in your sentence.**

_____

_____

Name _____

Point of View

The narrator is the person who is telling the story. A story can be told from different points of view, depending on who the narrator is.

- In first-person point of view, the narrator is a part of the story. This narrator uses words such as *I, me,* and *we.*

- In third-person point of view, the narrator is outside of the story. This narrator uses words such as *he, she,* and *they.*

> **Answer the questions about pages 113–114 of *Dear Primo*.**

1. Who is this story about?

_____

_____

2. How does the author tell the story?

_____

_____

3. So, who is the narrator of this story?

_____

_____

4. Do the cousins write in third-person or first-person? What words help you know this?

_____

_____

Name _____

More Long o Spellings

▶ **Read each sentence. Read the long *o* vowel or vowel team below the blank. Then find a word from the word bank that contains that vowel or vowel team and makes sense in the sentence. Write it in the blank.**

o	ow	oe	oa
folded colt	meadow sowed	tiptoed backhoe	goal toads

1. I _____ past the baby's room so I would not wake him.

　　　oe

2. Mike scored the winning _____ for his team.

　　　　　　　　　　　　oa

3. The pond is home to animals, such as turtles, ducks, and _____ .

　　　　　　　　　　　　　　　　　　　　　　　oa

4. I _____ my clothes and made my bed.

　　　o

5. The lively little _____ trotted with its mother in the _____ .

　　　　　　　　o　　　　　　　　　　　　　　　　ow

6. The _____ cleared the rocks from the field, and then the farmer _____

　　　oe　　　　　　　　　　　　　　　　　　　　　　　　　　　ow

the seeds.

Prefixes *re-* and *pre-*

A **prefix** is a word part added to the beginning of a base word that changes the meaning of the word.

▶ **Add either *re-* or *pre-* to each of the base words in the word bank to complete the sentences below.**

study   draw   visit   purchase   game   teen

1. During the _____ meeting, our coach decides who will play each position on the field.

2. If you _____ tickets, you won't have to stand in line for the movie.

3. I'm going to _____ this part of the lesson because I didn't understand it the first time.

4. My brother is only a _____ , but he tries to act like he's much older.

5. Benny will _____ his horse picture because the first one looked like a moose.

6. Charlotte took a short trip to see her friends, and she hopes to

_____ them soon.

Name _____

Text and Graphic Features

Some stories include **text features**, such as **bold** text and *italic* text. Punctuation, such as ellipses and dashes, can be text features, too.

Many stories include **graphic features** such as illustrations and labels.

▶ **Answer the questions about pages 122–123 of *Dear Primo*.**

1. How does the author make the Spanish words stand out?

_____

_____

2. Where else do the Spanish words appear?

_____

_____

3. How do the illustrations and labels help readers understand the meanings of the Spanish words?

_____

_____

_____

Name _____

Characters

Characters are the people and animals in a story. You can learn about characters through their traits, feelings, motivations, and responses. A character's **perspective** is his or her attitude toward something.

> **Answer the questions about pages 126–127 of *Dear Primo*.**

1. How is the weather alike where both boys live?

_____

2. What is each character's perspective on the weather? How do they respond to it?

_____

_____

3. What do the different settings tell you about the way each boy cools off?

_____

_____

> **Answer the questions about pages 138–140 of *Dear Primo*.**

4. How have the boys been learning about each other until now?

_____

5. How has this changed their relationship with each other?

_____

_____

6. What does the illustration on page 140 show you about the setting and plot events?

_____

_____

Name _____

More Long *i* Spellings

▶ **Read each sentence. Underline the word in each sentence with a long *i* sound. Circle the letters in each word that stand for the long *i* sound.**

1. Ben sighed when he discovered he had forgotten his homework.

2. You don't need a heavy coat when the weather is mild.

3. The baby cries loudly when she feels sleepy.

4. There were no seats left on the morning flight to Dallas.

5. The class read a fable about a sly fox who wanted some cheese.

6. Jean read an interesting book by a very famous author.

7. This path winds through the woods and around a lake.

8. The boy ate fried clams and chips on a visit to the seashore.

9. We had a slight change of plans when our car broke down.

10. The chorus will sing at a holiday concert on Friday.

Critical Vocabulary

You can use the words you learn from reading as you talk and write.

▶ **Read each sentence. Circle the letter beside the sentence that best fits the meaning of the word in bold print.**

1. desires

   a. Lena plans to take swimming lessons and play baseball.

   b. Lena dreams of climbing a mountain and learning to ski.

2. entry

   a. Roland wrote a note to thank his grandmother for his present.

   b. Roland wrote in his journal about the fun he had at his party.

▶ **Use both of the Critical Vocabulary words in a sentence. Include clues to each word's meaning in your sentence.**

_____

_____

Name _____

Elements of Poetry

Poems can be set up in special ways. **Stanzas** are groups of lines. Lines might include a specific number of syllables or might vary in length.

Poems use sounds in special ways. A **rhyme scheme** is the rhyming pattern at the ends of the lines.

▷ **Answer the questions about page 147 of *Adventures with Words*.**

1. Which words rhyme in "There was an Old Man with a Beard"?

_____

2. What rhyme scheme does the poem have? What kind of poem has this rhyme scheme?

_____

3. What other element of a limerick does this poem have?

_____

4. What type of poem is "My Journal"? How do you know?

_____

_____

▷ **Answer the questions about pages 148–150 of *Adventures with Words*.**

5. How does the shape of "In the Land of Words" match the ideas in the poem?

_____

6. How is a similar image created in "I Go to the Land" on page 150?

_____

7. What form are each of these poems? How do you know?

_____

More Long *i* Spellings

▶ **Read each clue. Unscramble the letters and write the word that answers the clue. Read the words you made.**

1. When you get a message, you might do this. lprey _____

2. You might use this after you clean your clothes in a washing machine. ryedr _____

3. This word can describe a powerful lion. ygmith _____

4. This is another word for *author*. itrerw _____

5. If you are neat and orderly, you are this. diyt _____

6. This tower can warn ships at sea. hoeislguth _____

7. This is what you do if you loosen your shoelaces. intue _____

8. This describes something that is not far away. rbenya _____

9. An acrobat can perform on this. opithtreg _____

10. This describes beans that you fry, and then fry again. freidre _____

Name _____

Critical Vocabulary

You can use the words you learn from reading as you talk and write.

▷ Use what you learned about the Critical Vocabulary words from
The Upside Down Boy **to help you complete each sentence.**

1. We were happy it was **breezy** out because _____ .

2. The job of the **conductor** is to help the group _____ .

3. When I have to climb a **steep** hill, I know it will be _____ .

4. If drivers **speed**, they might _____ .

▷ Write a sentence using two of the Critical Vocabulary words. Include
clues to each word's meaning in your sentence.

_____

_____

Name _____

Figurative Language

Figurative language helps readers imagine the author's ideas, or creates a special effect.

- A **simile** compares two things using the word *like* or *as*.

- A **metaphor** compares two things without using *like* or *as*. It often has the word *is* or *are*.

▶ **Answer the questions about page 161 of *The Upside Down Boy*.**

1. What similes does the author use in paragraphs 14 and 15?

_____

2. What are these similes comparing?

_____

_____

_____

3. In paragraph 17, what does Juanito call his tongue?

_____

4. Is his tongue really a rock?

_____

5. What does that metaphor mean?

_____

_____

Name _____

> **Answer the questions about pages 164–165 of *The Upside Down Boy*.**

6. When Juanito gets ready to sing, he says, "I am frozen." What does he mean?

_____

7. Do Juanito's eyes really open as big as the ceiling? What does the expression mean?

_____

8. What does Juanito mean when he says, "My hands spread out as if catching rain drops from the sky"?

_____

_____

Prefix dis-

A **prefix** is a word part added to the beginning of a base word that changes the meaning of the word.

▷ **Add the prefix *dis–* to words from the word bank to fill in the blanks in the story below.**

appear	organized	trust	approve	infect	satisfied

I am not the neatest person. In fact, I am very _____ , and my room is often a mess. Sometimes I can't find things I really need, like a school book, or a sneaker, or my lunch. The items seem to

_____ completely! Then a few days later I find them buried under a pile of papers or clothes.

My parents strongly _____ of my bad habits. They

told me they may need to wash and _____ all my belongings. I promised I would do a big cleanup. My words left them

_____ , though. They said, "Less talk, more action!"

I don't want them to _____ me. So I'll be in my room, cleaning, all weekend. I hope I can see my floor again soon.

Text and Graphic Features

Some stories include **text features** such as **bold** text and *italic* text. Punctuation, such as ellipses and dashes, can be used as text features, too.

Many stories include **graphic features** such as illustrations.

▶ **Answer the questions about pages 158–159 of *The Upside Down Boy*.**

1. What do you notice about the words in italics?

_____

2. How do you know the meanings of the Spanish words and phrases in this story?

_____

_____

_____

3. Why do you think the author includes the Spanish words?

_____

▶ **Answer the questions about pages 162–163 of *The Upside Down Boy*.**

4. Where is Juanito in the illustration?

_____

5. In the story, is Juanito really floating above the school, upside down?

_____

6. How does this picture help you understand the text?

_____

_____

7. Does Juanito like the feeling of floating? Use text evidence to justify your answer.

_____

_____

Name _____

Review Short and Long Vowels

> Read each sentence. Identify the vowel sound in the boldfaced word.
Underline the letter or letters that make the vowel sound in the word.
Circle the vowel sound below the sentence.

1. It's a good day to fly a **kite**.
   short *i*   long *i*   short *e*   long *e*

2. How much does that pumpkin **weigh**?
   short *e*   long *a*   long *e*   long *i*

3. Kim and I are **best** friends.
   short *e*   long *e*   short *a*   long *a*

4. That was a **huge** thunderstorm!
   short *e*   short *u*   long *e*   long *u*

5. Please go to the store to get some **milk**.
   short *e*   short *a*   long *e*   short *i*

6. Lia **reached** out to catch the ball.
   short *e*   long *a*   long *e*   short *a*

7. You need a heavy **coat** on this cold morning.
   short *o*   long *o*   short *a*   long *a*

8. **That** is the correct answer.
   short *i*   long *e*   long *a*   short *a*

9. Fireworks **shot** into the sky.
   long *o*   short *o*   long *a*   short *e*

10. I **must** get home before three o'clock.
    short *u*   long *u*   short *a*   long *a*

Name _____

Critical Vocabulary

You can use the words you learn from reading as you talk and write.

> **Use what you learned about the Critical Vocabulary words from** *Dear Dragon* **to help you complete each sentence.**

1. _____ is **precious** to me because _____ .

2. One reason for the **demolition** of a building is _____ .

3. Albert collected _____ to create his **mosaics**.

4. My favorite school **projects** are _____ .

5. One thing our school **retains** from year to year is _____ .

6. The last thing my teacher **assigned** is _____ .

> **Choose two of the Critical Vocabulary words and use them in a sentence.**

_____

_____

Name _____

Characters

Characters are the people and animals in a story. You can learn about characters through their traits, feelings, motivations, and responses. A character's **perspective** is his or her attitude toward something.

> **Answer the questions about pages 186–189 of *Dear Dragon*.**

1. How are George and Blaise alike? How are they different?

_____

_____

2. What is each character's perspective on the pen pal project so far?

_____

_____

3. What do the illustrations show about each character's perspective of the other?

_____

_____

_____

> **Answer the questions about pages 200–201 of *Dear Dragon*.**

4. How has sending letters to a pen pal changed Blaise and George?

_____

5. This is the first time in the story when we see both boys reading a letter at the same time. Why does the author do that?

_____

6. How can you tell they like each other?

_____

_____

7. How has each character's perspective about writing changed?

_____

_____

Name _____

Suffixes –y, –ly

A **suffix** is a word part added to the end of a base word that changes the meaning of the word.

The suffix –y changes a base word into an adjective. The suffix –ly changes a base word into an adverb that explains how or when something is done.

When you add either –y or –ly to a base word, the base word's spelling may change slightly. To add the suffix –y to a base word ending in e, you may need to drop the final e before adding the suffix. To add the suffix –ly to a base word ending in y, you need to replace the final y with i before adding the suffix.

> Add either –y or –ly to each of the base words in the word bank, and then use the new words to complete the paragraph.

cozy   rain   bare   speed   easy   mist

Dark clouds gathered above, and the air was _____ , like a thick

gray soup. I knew _____ weather was on its way. If I squinted

through the fog, I could _____ make out my house in the

distance. It's a good thing I'm a _____ runner. I knew I'd

_____ reach home before the downpour began. Then I could

cuddle up _____ with my cat and wait for the storm to end.

Name _____

Elements of Poetry

Poems can be set up in special ways.

- **Stanzas** are groups of lines.

- A **rhyme scheme** is the rhyming pattern at the ends of the lines.

▸ **Answer the questions about pages 184–187 of *Dear Dragon*.**

1. How are the pen pals' letters like poems?

_____

_____

2. How are the parts of each letter like the parts of a poem?

_____

_____

3. How are the stanzas similar in each letter?

_____

_____

_____

_____

Name _____

Review Short and Long Vowels

▶ **Read each sentence. Choose a word from the word bank that makes sense in the sentence. Write it in the blank. Then draw a line between the two syllables in the word you wrote.**

respect	students	moment	clever
raisins	silent	limit	polished

1. I _____ the silver platter so that it shined.

2. There are 20 _____ in our class.

3. When you are polite to other people you show them _____ .

4. I could not figure out the magician's _____ trick.

5. We made it inside just a _____ before it began to rain.

6. Max does not like _____ in his cereal.

7. No one was talking in the _____ library.

8. Big trucks can't drive over the bridge because it has a weight _____ .

Name _____

Point of View

Point of view is the answer to this question: *Who is telling the story?* It may be a narrator who is

- part of the story. This narrator uses words such as *I, me,* and *we.*
- outside of the story. This narrator uses words such as *he, she,* and *they.*

> **Answer the questions about pages 180–187 of *Dear Dragon*.**

1. Who has written the text on pages 181 and 182?

_____

2. How do you know?

_____

_____

3. Are the pen pals' letters written in first-person or third-person point of view?

_____

4. Which words are clues to the point of view?

_____

Name _____

Three-Letter Blends

> Read each question and choose an answer from the word bank.
Write the word.

scream	squid	street
strum	square	sprain
scrub	split	sprout

1. What is another word for *road*? _____

2. What do you do when you divide something into parts? _____

3. What kind of shape has four sides? _____

4. What will you see after you plant a seed? _____

5. What might you call a twisted ankle? _____

6. What would you call a very loud yell? _____

7. What do you call the relative of an octopus? _____

8. What is the best way to get dirty hands clean? _____

9. How might you play a guitar? _____

Name _____

Critical Vocabulary

You can use the words you learn from reading as you talk and write.

> **Use details and ideas from *The U.S. Constitution* to answer the questions.**

1. Why do we say that the U.S. Constitution is a **domestic** document?

_____

_____

2. Why is **tranquility** something we want for our country?

_____

_____

3. Why might you ask **delegates** to go to a **convention**?

_____

_____

4. Why do you think the authors thought about **posterity** when writing the U.S. Constitution?

_____

_____

5. What is one way to show concern for the **welfare** of others?

_____

_____

> **Choose two of the Critical Vocabulary words and use them in a sentence.**

_____

Name _____

Central Idea

The **central idea** is what a text is mostly about. Clues such as headings and visuals help readers identify the central idea. Facts and other relevant details provide evidence to support the central idea.

> **Answer the questions about page 231 of *The U.S. Constitution*.**

1. What is the central idea on page 231?

_____

_____

2. What details in the text support the central idea?

_____

_____

_____

> **Choose another section of *The U.S. Constitution*.**

3. What is the central idea?

_____

_____

4. What details in the text support that central idea?

_____

_____

Name _____

Three-Letter Blends

▶ **Read each sentence. Underline the word in each sentence that has a three-letter blend. Circle the blend in each word.**

1. The queen's splendid jewels glowed in her golden crown.

2. The toddler made a towering structure with blocks.

3. Carmen got a splinter in her finger when she painted the wooden fence.

4. Watch the diver leap gracefully from the edge of the springboard.

5. Luis scrolled through the text messages on his phone.

6. Studying for a test can be stressful sometimes.

7. The sculptor inscribed her name on the stone statue.

8. A squadron of aircraft flew overhead.

9. A salesperson can use a spreadsheet to keep track of his customers.

10. The cook made scrambled eggs and toast for breakfast.

Name _____

Suffixes –y, –less; Prefix dis–

A **suffix** is a word part added to the end of a base word that changes the meaning of the word. A **prefix** is a word part added to the beginning of a base word that changes the meaning of the word.

▶ **Add the suffix –y or –less or the prefix dis– to the words below to form words that complete each sentence.**

> like   curve   shoe   agree   grain   soap

1. I use lots of _____ water to wash my dog.

2. Don't give Nick and Trey any pickles because they both _____ sour foods.

3. Remember to go _____ in the house so the floors don't get dirty.

4. This trail is very _____ and loops around the mountain three times.

5. If you _____ with me, you're probably wrong.

6. The _____ beach sand is still stuck between my toes.

Text Structure

Text structure is the way information is organized in a text. Authors use transition words to provide clues to the structure.

> **Answer the questions about pages 227–228 of *The U.S. Constitution*.**

1. How has the author organized the information: by cause-effect, problem-solution, or chronology? How do you know?

_____

2. Why has the author used the text structure of chronology in this section?

_____

_____

_____

> **Choose another section of *The U.S. Constitution*.**

3. How has the author organized the information?

_____

_____

4. Why has the author used that text structure in this section?

_____

_____

Text and Graphic Features

Authors of informational text use **text features**, such as labels and headings, to further explain the information in the text. They use **graphic features**, such as illustrations, to help explain ideas in the text.

▶ **Answer the questions about pages 231–232 of *The U.S. Constitution*.**

1. How does the illustration on page 231 connect to the main text?

_____

_____

_____

2. How does the text in the blue box connect to the rest of the text?

_____

_____

_____

3. In the illustration on page 232, what do the labels name?

_____

_____

4. How does this illustration help you understand the text?

_____

_____

_____

Name _____

Words with /j/, /k/, and /kw/

▶ Write the word from the word bank that best replaces the underlined word or words in each sentence.

trudge	calf	gems
quit	pages	queen
core	strange	hedge

1. The <u>king's wife</u> lived in the castle. _____

2. How many <u>sheets of paper</u> are in this notebook? _____

3. Mr. Brown displays <u>jewels</u> in his shop window. _____

4. I will cut out the <u>center part</u> of the apple before I eat it. _____

5. The <u>young cow</u> stayed close to its mother. _____

6. Dad trims the <u>row of shrubs</u> each month. _____

7. Don't <u>stop</u> before you finish the job! _____

8. The cat was behaving in a very <u>odd</u> way. _____

9. We had to <u>walk slowly</u> through the deep snow. _____

Critical Vocabulary

You can use the words you learn from reading as you talk and write.

> **Read each pair of sentences. Circle the letter of the sentence that best fits the meaning of the Critical Vocabulary word in dark print.**

1. independence

   a. The teacher assigns each student a library book to read in class.

   b. The teacher lets her students choose the library books they want to read.

2. presented

   a. Javier was given an award at the school assembly.

   b. Lydia went to the school assembly with her parents.

3. declaring

   a. The principal is announcing the new rules for the playground.

   b. The principal is talking with some teachers in the hallway.

4. endowed

   a. The city put in new sidewalks all around our school.

   b. The large company gave our school money for new computers.

> **Choose two of the Critical Vocabulary words and use them in a sentence. Include clues to each word's meaning in your sentence.**

_____

_____

Name _____

Media Techniques

Authors use media to inform, entertain, and persuade viewers. **Media techniques**, such as sound elements, animation, and live action, are the ways a topic, an idea, or other information is presented.

▷ **Answer the questions about the video** *Why We Celebrate the Fourth of July.*

1. What images show pride in our country?

_____

_____

_____

2. How do sound techniques add to this feeling of pride, or patriotism?

_____

_____

_____

3. How do the paintings of scenes from the time of the Revolutionary War help you understand the information?

_____

_____

_____

Name _____

Words with /j/, /k/, and /kw/

▶ Read each sentence. Choose the missing word from the word bank. Write the word. Then reread the completed sentence.

garage	picnic	quarters
camera	gerbil	footbridge
fidget	quarrel	engine

1. A pet _____ likes to eat seeds.

2. I would love to drive a fire _____ !

3. The young children fuss and _____ if they get bored.

4. I will give you four _____ for a dollar bill.

5. Lin uses the _____ to cross the busy avenue.

6. You can take great photos with this new _____ .

7. The beach is a nice place to have a _____ .

8. The friends had a _____ over who won the game.

9. Tom parks his motorcycle in the _____ .

Critical Vocabulary

You can use the words you learn from reading as you talk and write.

▶ **Read each sentence. Circle the letter next to the sentence that best fits the meaning of the Critical Vocabulary word in dark print.**

1. hoisted

   a. At dawn, the boy raised the flag over the fort.

   b. At dusk, the boy lowered the flag down the pole.

2. broad

   a. The old street was too narrow for the car.

   b. The width of the bridge could hold several cars.

3. gritty

   a. Strong winds blew dust and dirt into the soldiers' faces.

   b. Strong winds blew garbage and dirt down the street.

▶ **Write a sentence using two of the Critical Vocabulary words. Include clues to each word's meaning in your sentence.**

_____

_____

Name _____

Text Structure

Text structure is the way information is organized in a text. Authors use transition words to provide clues to the structure.

> **Answer the questions about pages 252–253 of *The Flag Maker*.**

1. How is the text in this section organized? How do you know?

_____

_____

_____

_____

2. How does knowing the text structure help you understand what is happening?

_____

_____

_____

_____

_____

Suffixes –er and –est

A **suffix** is a word part added to the end of a base word that changes the meaning of the word.

The suffixes –*er* and –*est* are added to adjectives. The suffix –*er* is used to compare two things. The suffix –*est* is used to compare three or more things.

▶ **Add the suffix –*er* or –*est* to the word in parentheses to complete each sentence.**

1. My dog has a loud bark, but Suzi's dog has a (loud) _____ bark.

2. There are many tall buildings in the city, but that one is the (tall) _____ by far.

3. You've had a lot of crazy ideas, but this one is the (crazy) _____ you've ever had!

4. Which of these two sweaters is (ugly) _____ than the other?

5. The (rare) _____ of all birds is sitting in that tree.

6. For some people, math is (easy) _____ than reading.

Name _____

Content-Area Words

Authors of informational text often use **content-area words**, or words that are specific to the topic they are writing about. Social studies, science, and math texts all contain content-related words.

▶ **Answer the questions about page 254 of *The Flag Maker*.**

1. What do you think *ramparts* are?

_____

_____

2. What clues in the text help you figure out the meaning?

_____

_____

3. How does the illustration also help you with the meaning?

_____

_____

▶ **Answer the questions about page 257 of *The Flag Maker*.**

4. What do you think an *invasion* is? How can you tell?

_____

_____

5. What other words on this page have to do with fighting against an invading enemy?

_____

_____

Name _____

Silent Letters (*kn, wr, gn, mb, rh*)

▶ **Read each sentence. Choose the missing word from the word bank. Write the word. Then reread the complete sentence.**

knit	wring	gnaw
limb	rhythm	knight
reigns	wrong	comb

1. If you listen to lively music, you can't help but dance to the _____ .

2. A king _____ best from his throne in the castle.

3. To fight a pesky dragon, call a strong and fearless _____ .

4. If you see a dead _____ on a tree, call an expert to saw it off.

5. To make a wet sponge dry, you need to _____ it out.

6. If your hair is messy, you'd better find a brush or a _____ .

7. To get the answers right, not _____ , remember what you're taught.

8. To give a dog a treat, offer it a bone to _____ on.

9. If you want to _____ a scarf, get two needles and some yarn.

Critical Vocabulary

You can use the words you learn from reading as you talk and write.

▶ **Read the vocabulary word in the center of each word web. Then write words and phrases in the outer ovals that are related to the vocabulary word in the center.**

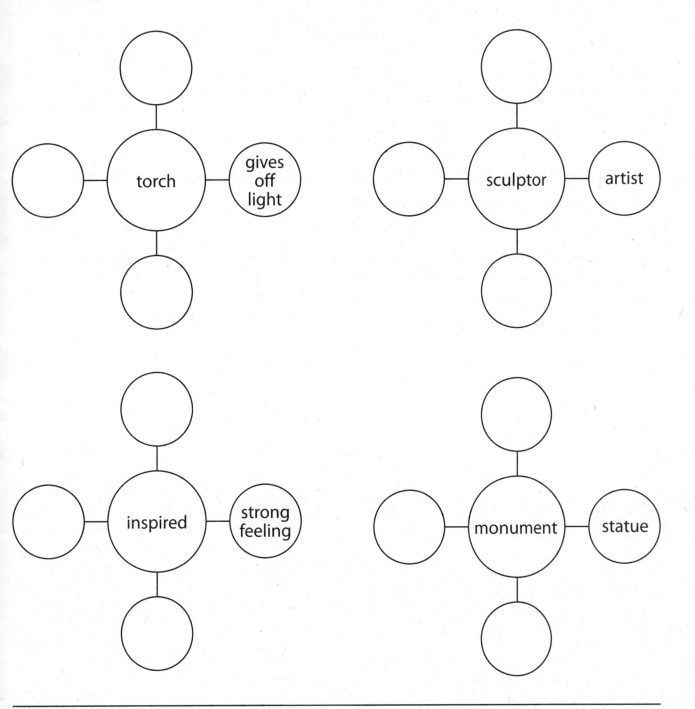

torch — gives off light

sculptor — artist

inspired — strong feeling

monument — statue

Name _____

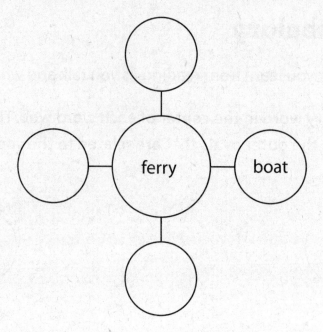

> Write a sentence using two of the Critical Vocabulary words. Include clues to each word's meaning in your sentence.

_____

_____

Name _____

Central Idea

The **central idea** is what a text is mostly about. Clues such as headings and visuals help readers identify the central idea. Facts and other relevant details provide evidence to support the central idea.

▶ **Answer the questions about page 279 of *Why Is the Statue of Liberty Green?***

1. What is the central idea of paragraph 29?

_____

_____

2. What relevant details about Ellis Island support the central idea?

_____

_____

3. Compare and contrast the way information about important monuments is presented in *American Places, American Ideals* and this text.

_____

_____

_____

_____

▶ **Choose another section of *Why Is the Statue of Liberty Green?***

4. What is the central idea? What relevant details support the central idea?

_____

_____

_____

Name _____

Prefix im-

A **prefix** is a word part added to the beginning of a base word that changes the meaning of the word.

▶ **Add the prefix *im–* to words from the word bank to fill in the blanks in the story below.**

possible   patient   polite   balance   movable

Zeke was pacing back and forth and tapping his foot. He had been waiting for

Amos a long time and was getting _____ . Amos tried to hurry,

but it was _____ to get his chores done any faster.

"I don't think this is quite fair," Amos finally said to Zeke. "There is an

_____ of work here. You finished cleaning your half of the

basement first because you only had to get rid of the old toys. I have to deal

with all these heavy boxes. Some of them are _____ !"

Zeke said, "I'm sorry. That was _____ of me. I'll help you

move the boxes."

Amos thought to himself, "Why didn't I ask him three hours ago?"

Name _____

Author's Purpose

The **author's purpose** is his or her reason for writing a text. Authors write to share an idea or a message.

▶ **Answer the questions about page 272 of *Why Is the Statue of Liberty Green?***

1. What is the author's purpose for writing this selection?

_____

_____

_____

_____

2. How does the author develop her purpose through Ranger Alisha?

_____

_____

_____

_____

Silent Letters (kn, wr, gn, mb, rh)

▸ Read each word in the word bank, and circle the consonant digraph with silent letters. Then read each clue. Write a word from the box that answers the clue.

foreign	wriggling	playwright
kneepads	rhino	thumbtack
redesign	honeycomb	knuckle

1. where bees store their food   _____

2. a pin to use on a bulletin board   _____

3. outside your own country   _____

4. a very large African mammal with horns rising from
   its snout   _____

5. how a snake could be moving   _____

6. a part of your finger   _____

7. a person who writes dramas   _____

8. come up with a new plan   _____

9. protective gear worn by a skateboarder   _____

Name _____

Literary Elements

Literary elements are the pieces that make up a story.

- **Characters** are the people and animals in a story.
- The **setting** is where and when the story takes place.
- **Plot** is the events that happen in a story.

▶ **Answer the questions about page 278 of** *Why Is the Statue of Liberty Green?*

1. What is different about the setting at this point in the field trip?

_____

_____

2. What details in the text help you picture the setting?

_____

_____

3. How is this setting different from and similar to the first setting of the story?

_____

_____

_____

_____

_____

Consonant Digraphs

> Read each clue. Write the word from the word bank that matches each clue.

| photo | chew | spring | thumb |
| stitch | cash | why | |

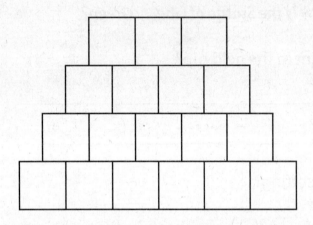

1. a question word

2. use your teeth

3. take it with a camera

4. sew with thread

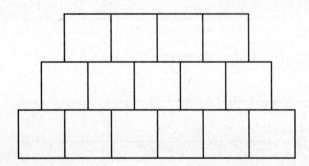

5. money

6. part of your hand

7. season after winter

Name _____

Critical Vocabulary

You can use the words you learn from reading as you talk and write.

▶ **Use details and ideas from *The Saga of Pecos Bill* to answer each question.**

1. Why does young Bill think he is a **genuine** coyote?

_____

_____

2. What may have happened if Bill had not **coiled** up the snake?

_____

_____

3. What is something that Pecos Bill is able to **tame**? How does he do it?

_____

_____

4. What happened when Pecos Bill **whirled** the rattlesnake?

_____

_____

5. What happens because of Pecos Bill's **saga** with the tornado?

_____

_____

▶ **Choose two of the Critical Vocabulary words and use them in a sentence.**

_____

_____

Name _____

Elements of Drama

A **drama** is a story performed by actors on a stage. Dramas, or plays, are written in a script. Drama scripts have special elements, such as the cast of characters and stage directions. Dramas are divided into acts and scenes.

▶ **Answer the questions about pages 298–299 of *The Saga of Pecos Bill.***

1. What features do you notice at the beginning of page 298? What is their purpose?

_____

_____

_____

2. In line 3, what are the first five words of dialogue and who is speaking them?

_____

_____

_____

3. Where does the play take place? How do you know?

_____

_____

_____

Consonant Digraphs

> Read each sentence. Underline the word in each sentence that has a consonant digraph. Circle the consonant digraph in each word.

1. Long ago, people traveled by stagecoach.

2. Val's homemade brownies vanished in no time at all.

3. Alice scored thirteen points in her basketball game.

4. Connor will celebrate his birthday at a water park.

5. My friends and I like to play checkers after school.

6. You can use a wheelbarrow to move soil in your garden.

7. Roberto has a hyphen in his last name.

8. Our mayor grasped every outstretched hand at her rally.

9. Joe's family got a kitten from an animal shelter.

10. My team runs six laps around an oblong track.

Name _____

Prefixes *in–* (not), *im–* (into)

A **prefix** is a word part added to the beginning of a base word that changes the meaning of the word.

▶ **Add the prefix *in–* (not) or *im–* (into) to base words from the word bank to complete each sentence.**

peril   complete   migrate   accurate   print   active

1. My pet mouse is _____ lately and won't use her running wheel.

2. The publisher will _____ the title in gold on the book cover.

3. Many people _____ to this country from other places.

4. Be careful to get the facts right so you don't say something _____ during the debate.

5. I don't know how to end the story I'm writing, so it is still _____ .

6. If you want to stay safe, don't _____ yourself by going skydiving!

Name _____

Literary Elements

Literary elements are the pieces that make up a story. The main literary elements in a story are the characters; the setting; the plot, which includes the conflict and resolution; and the events.

▶ **Answer the questions about pages 304–305 of** *The Saga of Pecos Bill.*

1. What big conflict does Pecos Bill have to deal with in this scene?

_____

_____

2. How do Bill's actions with the tornado lead to other events?

_____

_____

_____

_____

3. How is Bill's conflict with the tornado resolved?

_____

_____

_____

_____

_____

Name _____

Figurative Language

Figurative language is words or expressions that mean something different from their dictionary definitions. Examples of figurative language include imagery, hyperbole, and personification.

> **Answer the questions about page 302 of *The Saga of Pecos Bill*.**

1. What words does Narrator 3 repeat in line 33? What image do the words create? How?

_____

_____

2. What details make this scene a good example of hyperbole, or exaggeration?

_____

3. How is the language that Narrator 3 uses in line 36 different from the language in the Staging note in paragraph 1 on page 298?

_____

_____

> **Answer the questions about pages 304–305 of *The Saga of Pecos Bill*.**

4. What type of figurative language is used in lines 44-48? How do you know?

_____

_____

5. Why do you think this type of figurative language is used?

_____

Name _____

Vowel Diphthongs *ow, ou*

▶ Write a word from the word bank to answer each clue. Then use some letters in the word to answer the second clue. The letters may not be in the correct order.

howl	pouch	mouth	sprout
frown	brown	down	ground

1. not up __ __ __ __

right at this moment __ __ __

2. a kangaroo has one __ __ __ __ __

used for drinking __ __ __

3. a young plant's growth __ __ __ __ __ __

not bottom __ __ __

4. not a smile __ __ __ __ __

to move a boat with oars __ __ __

5. it holds your teeth __ __ __ __ __

sing with closed lips __ __ __

6. a sound a wolf can make __ __ __ __

not high __ __ __

7. the surface of Earth __ __ __ __ __ __

a carpet __ __ __

Name _____

Critical Vocabulary

You can use the words you learn from reading as you talk and write.

▶ **Use what you have learned about the Critical Vocabulary words from**
The Traveling Trio **video to help you finish each sentence.**

1. I can tell the theater was from the **Baroque** Period because

_____ .

2. The crew uses a **pulley** to lift parts of the set because _____ .

3. I would like to see a **performance** by _____ because

_____ .

4. The **backdrop** is important to the play because _____ .

▶ **Choose two of the Critical Vocabulary words and use them in a sentence.**
Include clues to each word's meaning in your sentence.

_____

_____

Name _____

Media Techniques

Authors use **media techniques** to present information in different ways. Some examples of media techniques are sound effects, graphics, live action, and animation.

▷ **Answer the questions about the video *The Traveling Trio*.**

1. How is the opening different from the rest of the video?

_____

_____

_____

_____

2. What sound techniques did you notice?

_____

_____

_____

_____

_____

3. Why do the video makers include these techniques?

_____

_____

_____

Vowel Diphthongs *ow, ou*

> ▶ **Read each sentence. Choose the missing word from the word bank. Write the word. Then reread the completed sentence.**

round	aloud	showers
rowdy	sunflower	fountain
outdoors	counter	towel

1. As soon as the rain stopped, the children hurried _____ to play.

2. Will it be a sunny day today, or will we have _____ ?

3. The teacher read a funny story _____ to the class.

4. If the children get too _____ , they might wake the baby.

5. The _____ seeds we planted grew into tall plants.

6. If you are thirsty, there is a water _____ in the hallway.

7. You will need a _____ after you take a bath.

8. A grapefruit and an orange have _____ shapes.

9. Please wipe the kitchen _____ with this sponge.

Critical Vocabulary

> Circle the letter of the sentence that best fits the meaning of the word in bold print.

1. superior

   a. Tanya has worked here longer than Brett, so she tells him what to do.

   b. Tanya often helps out Brett when he has too much work to do.

2. merciful

   a. The angry judge ordered the thief to go to jail.

   b. The understanding judge said anyone can make a mistake.

3. eminent

   a. The scientist is well known for her discoveries.

   b. The scientist worked alone in a small laboratory.

4. stately

   a. The small building was used for meetings.

   b. Fancy events were held in the large, beautiful home.

5. peasant

   a. The farmer grew a large crop to sell to many markets.

   b. The farmer worked hard but never had enough to eat.

6. deceive

   a. My sister tried to trick me into doing all her chores.

   b. My sister asked me to help her with her chores.

> Choose two of the Critical Vocabulary words and use them in a sentence.

_____

Name _____

Elements of Drama

A **drama** is a story performed by actors on a stage. Dramas, or plays, are written in a script. Drama scripts have special elements, such as the cast of characters and stage directions. Dramas are divided into acts and scenes.

▶ **Answer the questions about pages 321–326 of** *Gigi and the Wishing Ring.*

1. Which character sets up the scene?

_____

2. How do you know when the setting changes in this scene?

_____

_____

3. How did the events in Scene 2 with Old Woman lead to a problem for Gigi?

_____

_____

_____

▶ **Answer the questions about pages 328–329 of** *Gigi and the Wishing Ring.*

4. How do you know that Gigi is saved?

_____

5. How do the events at the end of Scene 4 resolve the problem in Scene 3?

_____

_____

_____

Suffixes –er and –or

A **suffix** is a word part added to the end of a base word that changes the meaning of the word.

▶ **Join each verb with the suffix *–er* or *–or* to make an adjective. Write the new word in the blank and give its meaning.**

1. create + or = _____

2. farm + er = _____

3. supervise + or = _____

4. dig + er = _____

5. heat + er = _____

6. inspect + or = _____

7. sin + er = _____

8. calculate + or = _____

Theme

A **theme** is the moral or lesson in a piece of writing. The theme is different from the topic. The topic is what the drama is about.

> **Answer the questions about page 330 of *Gigi and the Wishing Ring*.**

1. What lesson, or theme, about life does Gigi learn?

_____

_____

2. How does the author develop the theme throughout the text?

_____

_____

_____

_____

3. How is this theme different from the topic of the play?

_____

_____

_____

Name _____

Vowels au, aw, al, o

▶ Read each clue. Unscramble the letters and write the word that answers the clue. Read the words you made.

1. You could do a lot of shopping here.
lalm
_____

2. You will find these on a cat's paws.
wsacl
_____

3. This means the opposite of *right*.
gonwr
_____

4. You might do this if you felt tired.
aynw
_____

5. This is another word for *car*.
toau
_____

6. This is a place to keep money safe in a bank.
ltavu
_____

7. This means not true.
selaf
_____

8. This is a type of clothing to be worn around the shoulders.
lwash
_____

9. This is a clear soup.
otbhr
_____

10. This means without hair.
dlab
_____

Name _____

Critical Vocabulary

You can use the words you learn from reading as you talk and write.

▶ Read the vocabulary word in the center of each word web. Then write words and phrases in the outer circles related to the vocabulary word in the center. Discuss your word webs with a partner.

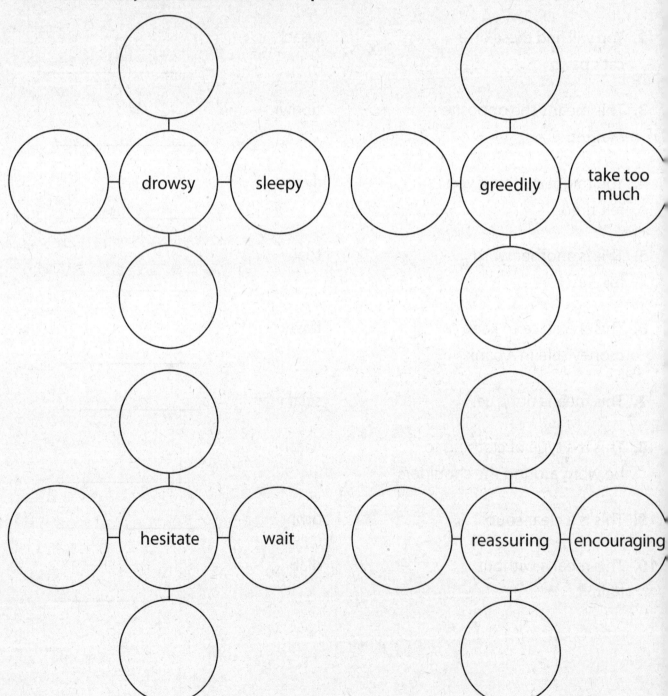

Name _____

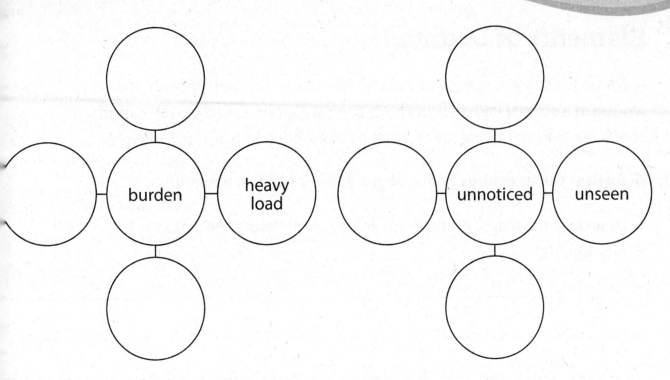

> **Choose two of the Critical Vocabulary words and use them in a sentence.**

_____

_____

Name _____

Elements of Drama

A **drama** is a story performed by actors on a stage. Dramas, or plays, are written in a script. Drama scripts have special elements, such as the cast of characters and stage directions. Dramas are divided into acts and scenes.

▶ **Answer the questions about pages 336–337 of *Two Bear Cubs*.**

1. How does the playwright provide information before the action in the play begins?

_____

_____

_____

2. How is the organization of this play similar to and different from *The Saga of Pecos Bill* and *Gigi and the Wishing Ring*?

_____

_____

_____

_____

_____

3. How does the Prologue connect to Scene 1?

_____

_____

_____

Name _____

Latin Roots aud, vis

A **root** is a basic word part, usually from Greek or Latin, that carries meaning. Knowing the meaning of roots can help you understand the meaning of many different words with the same root.

▷ **Choose a word from the word bank to complete each of the sentences below.**

| audio | visualize | audition | invisible | visit | auditorium |

1. The director watched Deval _____ for a role in the play.

2. We want to see our friends in Texas, so we are going to _____ them next week.

3. Sometimes I close my eyes and try to _____ my favorite place, and it's almost as if I can see it in front of me.

4. Our school's _____ was filled with students waiting to see the performance.

5. You need to adjust the _____ control if you want to make the music louder.

6. What if you had the power to be _____ and could come and go with no one seeing you?

Name _____

Literary Elements

Literary elements are the pieces that make up a story. The main literary elements in a story are the characters; the setting; the plot, which includes the conflict and resolution; and the events.

▷ **Answer the questions about pages 338–340 of _Two Bear Cubs._**

1. What happens to the setting when the bear cubs fall asleep?

_____

_____

2. What do the cubs do in Scene 1 that helps cause the change to the setting in Scene 2?

_____

_____

3. What conflict, or problem, does this cause for Mother Grizzly?

_____

_____

▷ **Answer the questions about pages 345–347 of _Two Bear Cubs._**

4. Who is finally able to resolve Mother Bear's problem?

_____

5. How does Measuring Worm succeed when the other animals fail?

_____

_____

Name _____

Vowels au, aw, al, o

 Read each question and choose an answer from the word bank. Write the word.

seesaw	office	sidewalk
softball	jigsaw	laundry
autumn	nightfall	halter

1. Where is a place you could roller skate?　　　　　_____

2. When do trees lose their leaves?　　　　　_____

3. What do you call a place where people can work?　　　　　_____

4. What is found on a playground for two children to ride?　　　　　_____

5. What time is it when the sun goes down?　　　　　_____

6. What kind of puzzle has many pieces?　　　　　_____

7. What is one sport that can be played on a diamond?　　　　　_____

8. What is a strap that fits over a horse's head called?　　　　　_____

9. What are clothes that need to be washed?　　　　　_____

Name _____

Theme

A **theme** is the moral or lesson in a piece of writing. The theme is different from the topic. The topic is what the drama is about.

▸ **Answer the questions about pages 347–348 of *Two Bear Cubs.***

1. What theme, or lesson about life, does the play give to readers?

_____

_____

2. How does the author develop the theme?

_____

_____

_____

_____

3. How is a lesson the cubs learn similar to one that Gigi learns in *Gigi and the Wishing Ring*?

_____

_____

_____

_____

Name _____

Vowel Sounds *oi*, *oy*

> Read each sentence. Look at the clue below the blank. Use the clue to help you choose a word from the word bank that makes sense in the sentence. Write it in the blank.

toy	coin	boy	point	joy
oil	spoils	join	soil	noise

1. The squeaky wheel needs some _____ .

oi

2. Put the food away before it _____ .

oi

3. Give the baby a fun _____ to play with.

oy

4. What was that loud _____ ?

oi

5. Ask Joyce if she is free to _____ us at the zoo.

oi

6. The little _____ turned three years old.

oy

7. Please _____ to our town on the map.

oi

8. We planted some seeds in the _____ .

oi

9. She dropped the _____ into her piggy bank.

oi

10. Singing gives me a feeling of great _____ .

oy

Grade 3

99

Module 5 • Week 1

Critical Vocabulary

You can use the words you learn from reading as you talk and write.

▶ **Read each sentence. Decide which sentence best fits the meaning of the word in bold print. Circle the letter next to that sentence.**

1. competition

  a. Let's race to the park to see who is faster.

  b. Let's play catch together in the park.

2. deflected

  a. Carlos rolled the beach ball to the baby, and the baby clapped her hands.

  b. Carlos saw the beach ball heading toward the baby and knocked it away.

3. technical

  a. I showed my sister all the basic moves for snowboarding.

  b. I cleaned off my snowboard and made sure it was dry.

4. apprehensive

  a. At the baseball game, I was cheering for the home team.

  b. At the baseball game, I was worried the home team would lose.

5. intercepted

  a. When Greg passed the basketball to Shelly, she shot it and scored.

  b. When Greg tried to pass the ball to Shelly, I grabbed it and passed it.

6. sprawling

  a. The goalkeeper reached out his arms and dove toward the ball.

  b. The goalkeeper ran forward and kicked the ball away from the net.

Name _____

Literary Elements

Literary elements are the pieces that make up a story. The main literary elements in a story are the characters; the setting; the plot, which includes the conflict and resolution; and the events.

▷ **Answer the questions about pages 364–366 of *Soccer Shootout*.**

1. Who are the major and minor characters? How are they different?

_____

_____

_____

2. How do the differences between Berk and Ryan influence the plot?

_____

_____

_____

3. What is the setting on these pages?

_____

_____

4. Why is this setting important for a story about soccer?

_____

_____

_____

Name _____

Vowel Sounds oi, oy

▶ **Read each sentence. Look for the word with missing letters. Write *oi* or *oy* in the blank to complete the word correctly.**

1. I woke up because of the n____sy workers outside my window.

2. Leila is a l____al friend whom I can always trust.

3. A trip around the world would be a v____age of a lifetime.

4. The rusty door hinge wouldn't open because no one had ____led it for years.

5. A queen is a r____al ruler.

6. It is best to av____d going outside in a thunderstorm.

7. I sharpened my pencil until the tip was p____nty.

8. Troy likes horseback riding because it makes him feel like a cowb____ .

9. If you enj____ funny movies, you will love this one!

10. Dad b____led water to make pasta.

Name _____

Suffixes –er, –or; –er, –est

A **suffix** is a word part added to the end of a base word that changes the meaning of the word.

▶ Add the suffix to each base word below to make a new word. Then use the words to finish the sentences.

1. ride + *er* = _____

2. profess + *or* = _____

3. pale + *er* = _____

4. pale + *est* = _____

5. silly + *er* = _____

6. silly + *est* = _____

1. The second joke was _____ than the first.

2. I've heard silly jokes before, but that is by far the _____ joke
I've ever heard.

3. Bonnie is an excellent bike _____ and wins lots of races.

4. Chaz is a college _____ who teaches chemistry.

5. This color is the _____ of all.

6. Of these two paint colors, which one is _____ ?

Name _____

Theme

A **theme** is the moral or lesson in a piece of writing.

> **Answer the questions about page 378 of *Soccer Shootout*.**

1. What is the theme of this story?

_____

_____

_____

_____

2. How does the author develop the theme throughout the story?

_____

_____

_____

_____

_____

_____

_____

Name _____

Author's Craft

Author's craft is the language and techniques a writer uses to make his or her writing interesting. Authors use voice, tone, mood, and word choice to create different effects. They may also use literal language to describe events.

▷ **Answer the questions about pages 376–377 of** *Soccer Shootout.*

1. What words could you use to describe the mood—the suggested feelings— in this part of the story?

_____

_____

2. How does the author use literal language, sensory words, and sentence length to describe the action? How does the author's word choice help to create the mood?

_____

_____

_____

_____

_____

3. What do these pages tell about the author's tone, or his feelings about the game of soccer?

_____

_____

Name _____

Homophones

▶ Read each sentence. Look at the homophones in bold print. Circle the homophones that makes sense in each sentence.

1. When I can't think of anything to do, I feel **bored/board**.

2. Has the grass in the yard been **moan/mown** yet?

3. We grew **beats/beets** in **our/hour** garden.

4. Jacob saw a **dear/deer** in the woods last **night/knight**.

5. The **be/bee** buzzed **hi/high** over my head.

6. I plan to **meet/meat** my cousin in one **our/hour**.

7. We **ate/eight** vegetables and **meet/meat** for dinner.

8. Do you **no/know** what the **some/sum** of **eight/ate** plus seven is?

9. Emma went to **by/buy/bye** a new **pair/pear/pare** of **shoos/shoes**.

10. The **sun/son shone/shown** on the waves at **see/sea**.

Name _____

Critical Vocabulary

You can use the words you learn from reading as you talk and write.

> Read the vocabulary word in the center of each word web. Then write words and phrases that are related to the Critical Vocabulary word in the outer ovals. Discuss your word webs with a partner.

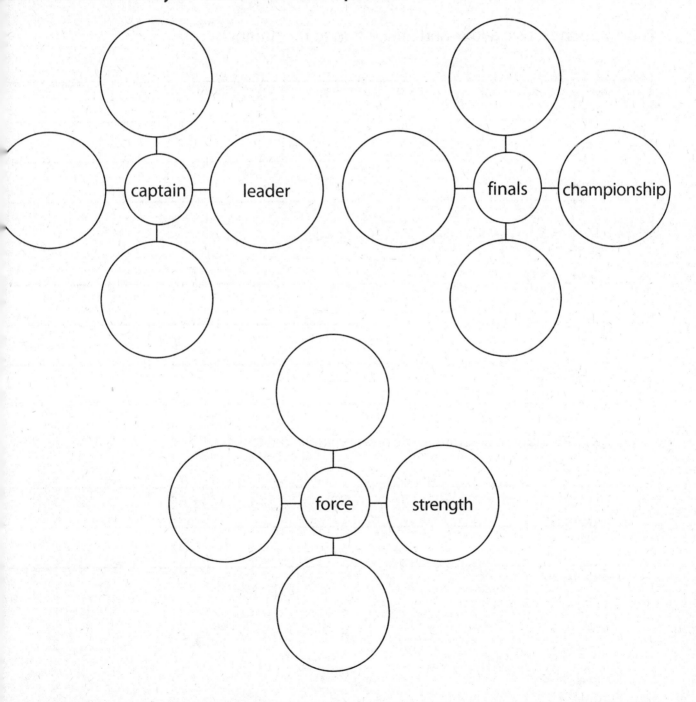

Name _____

Media Techniques

Authors use **media techniques** to present information in different ways. Some examples of media techniques are sound effects, graphics, live action, and animation.

> **Answer the questions about the video *Bend It Like Bianca.***

1. How do the music and sound effects add to the humor?

_____

_____

_____

_____

2. How do the visuals change during the video?

_____

_____

_____

_____

3. Why do the video makers use different visuals like this?

_____

_____

_____

Name _____

Homophones

> Read each sentence. Choose a homophone from the word bank that makes sense in the sentence. Write it in the blank. Reread the complete sentence.

bolder	ceiling	serial	flower
boulder	sealing	cereal	flour

1. Emily picked a pretty _____ for Mom.

2. A huge _____ blocked the mountain road.

3. A spider made a web high up on the _____ .

4. I ate a bowl of _____ with milk for breakfast.

5. The cake recipe calls for two cups of _____ .

6. Every week, Dan likes to listen to a _____ podcast about football.

7. If I were _____ , I would not be so nervous when I speak in front of the class.

8. Workers were _____ the windows so rain wouldn't get in.

Name _____

Critical Vocabulary

You can use the words you learn from reading as you talk and write.

> Use details and ideas from *Running Rivals* to support your answers to the questions below.

1. What could happen in a race that might **upset** a runner?

_____

_____

2. How might a runner feel about racing at a **personal** best during a **meet**?

_____

_____

3. What are some steps you took when you **concentrated** on learning something new?

_____

_____

4. Why might someone feel **disappointed** after a race?

_____

_____

> Write a sentence using two of the Critical Vocabulary words. Include clues to each word's meaning in your sentence.

_____

_____

Name _____

Literary Elements

Literary elements are the pieces that make up a story. The main literary elements in a story are the characters; the setting; the plot, which includes the conflict and resolution; and the events.

> **Answer the questions about page 393 of *Running Rivals*.**

1. Who are the major and minor characters in this chapter? How do you know?

_____

_____

_____

2. How is Natalie impacting the plot in this scene?

_____

_____

_____

> **Answer the questions about page 394 of *Running Rivals*.**

3. Why is the setting important for understanding the events in this chapter?

_____

_____

_____

4. In what way is Amy's relationship with Madison similar to Berk's relationship with Ryan in *Soccer Shootout*?

_____

Name _____

Greek Root *bio* and Latin Root *vid*

A **root** is a basic part added to the end of a base word that changes the meaning of the word.

▶ **Use words from the word bank to complete each sentence.**

autobiography   evident   biofuel   provide   biologist   videographer

1. The basketball film was made by a _____ who follows the team from game to game.

2. After her final trip, the explorer started writing her _____ to tell the story of her life.

3. Based on all the information we have seen, it is _____ that the cat destroyed your couch.

4. Some vehicles run on _____ , which is made from living organisms.

5. Exene is a _____ who studies whales and other mammals that live in the ocean.

6. I can see you need some groceries, so I'll be happy to _____ them.

Name _____

Author's Purpose

The **author's purpose** is his or her reason for writing a text. Authors write to share an idea or message.

▷ **Answer the questions about page 399 of *Running Rivals*.**

1. What is the author's purpose for writing this text?

_____

_____

_____

2. What is the author trying to show in this part of the story?

_____

_____

_____

_____

3. How does this chapter connect to the author's purpose in the last chapter?

_____

_____

_____

_____

Name _____

Contractions

> Read each sentence and contraction. Choose the contraction from the word bank that replaces the words in bold. Write it in the blank.

> they'd   you'd   I'd
> we've   I've

1. If I had to sleep in the woods, **I would** bring lots of bug spray.

_____

2. If you saw the movie, **you would** love it as much as I did.

_____

3. We haven't seen the movie, but **we have** both read the book.

_____

4. Personally, **I have** always admired Ben Franklin.

_____

5. If our friends saw us, **they would** be really surprised.

_____

> Read each sentence. Decode each contraction. Then write the two words for which the contraction is a shortened form.

6. I promise I **won't** tell your secret.

_____ _____

7. I'm sorry, I **can't** go to basketball practice.

_____ _____

8. Who **hasn't** turned in the math homework?

_____ _____

9. I **don't** know what time it is.

_____ _____

Name _____

Critical Vocabulary

You can use the words you learn from reading as you talk and write.

> **Read each sentence. Decide which sentence best fits the meaning of the word in bold print. Circle the letter next to that sentence.**

1. soared

   a. The eagle perched on a high branch.

   b. The eagle flew far above us.

2. rivalry

   a. Fazul and I both want to be class president this year.

   b. Fazul and I are working together to elect the class president.

3. littered

   a. Mark has a lot of space in his room for all his clothes, sneakers, and books.

   b. Mark's room is covered in clothes, sneakers, and books he never puts away.

4. generations

   a. My older and younger relatives gathered at the family reunion.

   b. My sisters and brothers came with me to the family reunion.

5. disbanded

   a. Our club got three new members this year.

   b. Our club split up at the end of the year.

6. donated

   a. We gave the school money for new band equipment.

   b. We asked when the school would have new band equipment.

Name _____

Figurative Language

Figurative language includes "figures of speech" that compare, exaggerate, or mean something different from what is expected. Figurative language also helps create a special effect or feeling. Examples of figurative language include imagery and onomatopoeia.

> **Answer the questions about page 419 of *Brothers at Bat*.**

1. What image does the author use to describe the Atlantic Ocean in paragraph 33?

_____

2. Is the Atlantic Ocean really like a stew that you would smell cooking on a stove?

_____

3. Why did the author choose to describe the Atlantic Ocean this way?

_____

_____

4. Which word in paragraph 34 is an example of onomatopoeia?

_____

5. Why does the author repeat the word?

_____

_____

_____

_____

Name _____

Suffix –ment

A **suffix** is a word part added to the end of a base word that changes the meaning of the word.

▶ **Add the suffix _–ment_ to verbs from the word bank to make nouns. Then use them to finish the sentences.**

measure   ship   replace   amaze   employ   disagree

1. I watched in surprise and _____ as my friend climbed to the top of the highest tree.

2. The store manager said she will receive a new _____ of skateboards today.

3. Britt and Germaine finally ended their _____ and decided to make peace with each other.

4. If you don't become an astronaut, what other kind of _____ are you interested in?

5. Our teacher is out sick, so a substitute teacher will be her _____ this week.

6. We need to get an accurate _____ , so be sure to use your ruler.

Name _____

Text Structure

Text structure is the way information is organized in a text. Authors use transition words to provide clues to the structure.

> **Answer the questions about pages 408–409 of *Brothers at Bat*.**

1. How does the author organize the events? How do you know?

_____

_____

2. Why might the author choose this text structure for narrative nonfiction?

_____

_____

3. How do the illustrations help you follow the structure on this page?

_____

_____

> **Answer the questions about pages 420–421 of *Brothers at Bat*.**

4. What is the structure of this part of the text? How do you know?

_____

_____

5. How does knowing the text structure help you understand what is happening?

_____

_____

_____

Name _____

Contractions

▶ Read each sentence. Choose the missing contraction from the word bank. Write it in the blank. Then reread the complete sentence.

aren't	what'd	mustn't
they'd	couldn't	wasn't
haven't	should've	might've

1. I _____ open the jar because the lid was too tight.

2. I realized I _____ practiced my trumpet more before the band concert.

3. Why are you serving us dessert when we _____ eaten dinner?

4. _____ have gone on a picnic today but didn't because of the heavy rain.

5. I _____ won the race, but my sneaker came untied.

6. Why _____ the door locked when we were out?

7. _____ you see at the zoo yesterday?

8. You _____ remove the bandage before the cut is healed.

9. My parents _____ too strict, but they do have some rules.

Name _____

Point of View

Point of view is the answer to this question: *Who is telling the story?* It may be a narrator who is:

- part of the story. This narrator uses words such as *I, me,* and *we.*
- outside of the story. This narrator uses words such as *he, she,* and *they.*

▶ **Answer the questions about page 410 of** *Brothers at Bat.*

1. Who is telling about the Acerra family—a narrator inside the text or a narrator outside the text?

_____

_____

2. So, is the text written in first-person or third-person point of view?

_____

_____

3. How can you tell?

_____

_____

_____

Name _____

Words with *ar, or, ore*

> ▶ Read each sentence. Find the word that has the /är/ or /ôr/ sound. Underline the letters that make the sound. After the sentence, circle /är/ or /ôr/.

1. Use a fork to eat your salad.

   /är/   /ôr/

2. We played kickball in the yard.

   /är/   /ôr/

3. I have a scar on my knee from the time I fell off my bike.

   /är/   /ôr/

4. You may harm the plants if you step on them.

   /är/   /ôr/

5. Ajit's head felt sore after he bumped it.

   /är/   /ôr/

6. The kitten played with a ball of yarn.

   /är/   /ôr/

7. My dad snores loudly when he sleeps.

   /är/   /ôr/

8. The car honked its horn at the stoplight.

   /är/   /ôr/

9. The window was stuck, so Maddy had to force it open.

   /är/   /ôr/

10. I made a birthday card for Mom.

    /är/   /ôr/

Name _____

Critical Vocabulary

You can use the words you learn from reading as you talk and write.

▶ **Use what you learned about the vocabulary words from** *This Is Your Life Cycle* **to help you finish each sentence.**

1. Dahlia's mom **deposited** her _____ .

2. Insects become **larvae** after they _____ .

3. When dragonfly nymphs **molt**, they _____ .

4. An **unsuspecting** tadpole was surprised when _____ .

5. Dahlia began her life in a **patch** of _____ .

6. After Dahlia shed her **cumbersome** exoskeleton, she

_____

▶ **Choose two of the Critical Vocabulary words and use them in a sentence. Include clues to each word's meaning in your sentence.**

_____

_____

Name _____

Author's Purpose

The **author's purpose** is his or her reason for writing a text. Authors may write to inform, entertain, or persuade the reader.

> **Answer the questions about page 18 of** *This Is Your Life Cycle.*

1. What is the topic of this text?

_____

_____

_____

2. What is the author's purpose for writing this text?

_____

_____

_____

3. How does the game show setting help the author develop her purpose?

_____

_____

_____

_____

_____

Name _____

Words with ar, or, ore

▶ Read each sentence. Look for the word with missing letters. Write *ar*, *or*, or *ore* in the blank to complete the word correctly.

1. I have to study for an imp____tant test.

2. The p____king lot was full, so we had to find another place to put the truck.

3. We grew carrots, beets, and lettuce in our g____den.

4. When my little brother makes noise, I just try to ign____ him.

5. The class enjoyed the information in my rep____t about the rainforest.

6. "Waiting in the dentist's office is b____ing," said Ava.

7. My pants were too long, so Mom sh____tened them.

8. In the summer, we go swimming at the seash____ .

9. David and Noah had an ____gument about which was the best basketball team.

10. We spent the day hiking in the f____est.

Name _____

Prefixes uni-, bi-, tri-

A **prefix** is a word part added to the beginning of a base word that changes the meaning of the word.

▶ **Add the prefix** *uni–*, *bi–*, **or** *tri–* **to complete the words below.**

1. Something with only one dimension is _____ dimensional.

2. An event that happens two times a year is _____ annual.

3. An imaginary animal with one horn in the middle of its head is called a

_____ corn.

4. A three-sided figure is called a _____ angle.

5. A dog that is black and white could be called _____ colored.

6. If something has three sections, it is _____ part.

Name _____

Text and Graphic Features

Authors of informational text use **text features** such as labels and headings to further explain the information in the text. They use **graphic features** such as illustrations and diagrams to help explain ideas in the text.

> **Answer the questions about pages 20–21 of *This Is Your Life Cycle*.**

1. What types of text features does the author use on these pages?

_____

_____

2. What kinds of information do these each give?

_____

_____

_____

3. How do the illustrations help show the author's purpose?

_____

_____

> **Answer the questions about page 33 of *This Is Your Life Cycle*.**

4. What text does the diagram connect to?

_____

_____

5. How does the diagram help you better understand the text?

_____

_____

Name _____

Author's Craft

Author's craft is the language and techniques a writer uses to make his or her writing interesting and to share ideas with the reader. Techniques include the author's **voice** and the **mood**, or the feelings and emotions of the reader while reading.

▶ **Answer the questions about page 36 of** *This Is Your Life Cycle.*

1. What is surprising about the tone of this section?

_____

_____

_____

2. Why are the illustrations and the text in paragraph 43 good clues to the author's voice?

_____

_____

_____

_____

_____

3. What words could describe the mood—the feelings created in the reader?

_____

_____

_____

Name _____

Words with er, ir, ur, or

▶ Read each sentence. Look at the word choices under the sentence. Write the correctly spelled word in the blank.

1. We can't wait to see the acrobats at the _____ .
   cercus   **circus**

2. I went to the school _____ because I scraped my knee
   at recess.
   nurse   **nerse**

3. Please _____ on your book report tonight.
   work   **wurk**

4. He was happy to win _____ prize for the triple jump.
   thurd   **third**

5. Take a left _____ at the stop sign.
   tern   **turn**

6. I could hear the _____ chirping early in the morning.
   birds   **burds**

7. The kitten has such soft _____ !
   fir   **fur**

8. Did she find _____ lost coat?
   her   **hir**

9. Please excuse yourself when you _____ .
   burp   **birp**

10. Where is the coldest place in the _____ ?
    wirld   **world**

Critical Vocabulary

You can use the words you learn from reading as you talk and write.

> Create a word web for each of the Critical Vocabulary words. In the center circle, write a Critical Vocabulary word. Then write words and phrases that are related to the Critical Vocabulary word in the outer circles. Discuss your word webs with a partner.

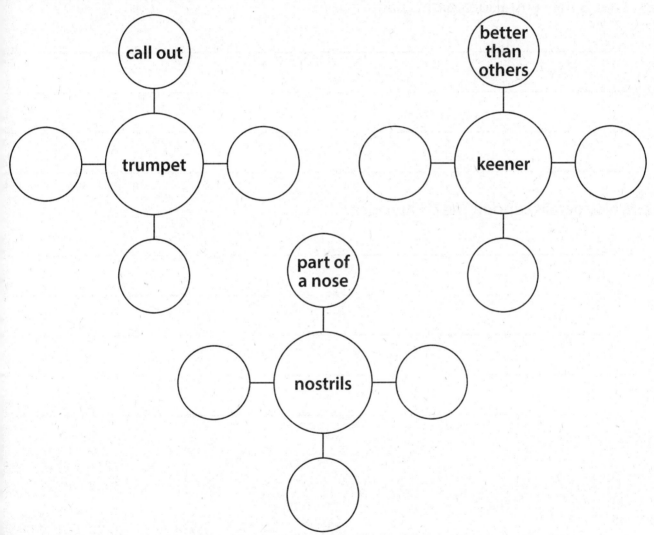

> Choose two of the Critical Vocabulary words and use them in a sentence. Include clues to each word's meaning in your sentence.

_____

_____

Name _____

Central Idea

The **central idea** is what a text is mostly about. Clues such as headings and visuals help readers identify the central idea. Facts and other details provide evidence to support the central idea.

▶ **Answer the questions about page 49 of *The Nose Awards*.**

1. What is the central idea of this page?

_____

_____

_____

_____

2. Which details support the central idea?

_____

_____

_____

_____

Name _____

Words with er, ir, ur, or

▶ **Write a word from the word bank to complete each sentence. Then read the sentence to make sure it makes sense.**

October	butterfly	burger
soccer	yogurt	murmured
certain	actor	burning

1. David is an _____ in a new play.

2. I ate a sandwich, fruit, and _____ for lunch.

3. The forest fire had been _____ for three days.

4. My favorite month is _____ when the weather gets cool.

5. The restaurant is known for having a great _____ and tasty fries.

6. Lindy's favorite sport is _____ .

7. A beautiful orange _____ landed on the leaf.

8. The students _____ with excitement as they waited for the surprise guest.

9. Are you _____ that you have the right answer to the math problem?

Name _____

Critical Vocabulary

You can use the words you learn from reading as you talk and write.

> **Use the word line to answer each question. Then explain your answer.**

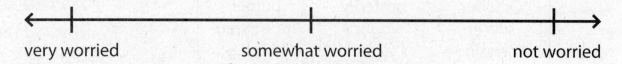

very worried   somewhat worried   not worried

How worried would you be if . . .

1. you saw a fox **lurking** in the bushes?

_____

_____

2. your straw was **flexible**?

_____

_____

3. you suddenly became **invisible**?

_____

_____

4. there was a hole in the **siphon**?

_____

_____

> **Write a sentence using two of the Critical Vocabulary words. Include clues to each word's meaning in your sentence.**

_____

_____

Name _____

Figurative Language

Figurative language is language that adds special effects to text and makes it more interesting. Imagery, sound devices, and repetition are examples of figurative language.

> **Answer the questions about page 59 of *Octopus Escapes Again!***

1. Which word has the author repeated?

_____

2. Why does the author repeat this word?

_____

3. How does the author change the type to make this repetition stand out?

_____

> **Answer the questions about pages 64–65 of *Octopus Escapes Again!***

4. What similes has the author used?

_____

5. How do the similes help readers form pictures in their minds?

_____

_____

> **Answer the question about page 68 of *Octopus Escapes Again!***

6. Which word is an example of onomatopoeia? Why does the author use this word here?

_____

_____

Name _____

Prefix un-

A **prefix** is a word part added to the beginning of a base word that changes the meaning of the word.

▶ **Add the prefix *un*– to words from the word bank. Then choose the best word to finish each sentence.**

certain   pleasant   embarrassed   related   friendly

1. I thought Jared was _____ because he doesn't talk much, but really he's just shy.

2. Marta is _____ to dance even though she says she's clumsy.

3. Our cats, Trixie and Tutu, look a lot alike, but they are _____ .

4. If you feel _____ about your homework, ask your teacher for help.

5. Georgia hates pickles and says they have an _____ taste.

Text and Graphic Features

Authors of informational text use **text features**, such as labels and sidebars, to further explain the information in the text. They use graphic features, such as illustrations and diagrams, to help explain ideas in the text.

▷ **Answer the questions about page 60 of** *Octopus Escapes Again!*

1. What are the two types of text on this page?

_____

2. What type of information does each type of text present?

_____

_____

3. How does the author play with punctuation in paragraph 7?

_____

_____

▷ **Answer the questions about page 70 of** *Octopus Escapes Again!*

4. How is the text on this page different from the rest of the text?

_____

5. How does the diagram connect to details in the text?

_____

_____

6. What added information is in the diagram that is not in the text?

_____

_____

Words with /âr/ and /îr/

> Read each sentence. Look at the word choices under the sentence. Write the correctly spelled word in the blank.

1. The sky was _____ blue with no clouds.
   clear   **clere**

2. I need a new _____ of socks because my old ones have holes.
   pare   **pair**

3. The baby _____ at my glasses.
   stared   **staired**

4. Please tell your sister to come _____ .
   here   **heer**

5. I _____ out the window to see who was coming up the street.
   peired   **peered**

6. That sure is a _____ hat you're wearing.
   weard   **weird**

7. Little statues of a bride and groom stood on the top _____ of the wedding cake.
   tier   **tere**

8. We watched a special show about the lives of _____ .
   bears   **bares**

9. _____ did Jenna and Lily go?
   Whear   **Where**

10. Liam _____ made it to school on time.
    neirly   **nearly**

Name _____

Critical Vocabulary

▷ Use details and ideas from *T.J. the Siberian Tiger Cub* to support your answers to the questions below.

1. What is one job that a veterinary **assistant** does?

_____

_____

2. How does the **nursery** staff know that T.J. is getting better?

_____

_____

3. Why had Buhkra **nuzzled** her new cub?

_____

_____

4. When might one animal **pounce** on another animal?

_____

_____

5. Buhkra always **bared** her teeth at Sheila. Why?

_____

_____

6. Why do you think T.J. **refused** to eat for such a long time?

_____

_____

Name _____

Text Structure

Text structure is the way information is organized in a text. Types of text structure include cause and effect, problem and solution, compare and contrast, and chronology.

> **Answer the questions about pages 76–77 of _T.J. The Siberian Tiger Cub._**

1. In paragraphs 1 and 2, how does the author organize the text? How do you know?

_____

_____

_____

2. Why do you think the author used this text structure?

_____

3. Which structure does the author use in paragraph 4? How do you know?

_____

_____

> **Answer the questions about page 82 of _T.J. The Siberian Tiger Cub._**

4. What happens in paragraph 15? What does this cause to happen?

_____

_____

5. What text structure does the author use in paragraph 15?

_____

Name _____

Suffix –*ly*

A **suffix** is a word part added to the end of a base word that changes the meaning of the word.

> **Add the suffix –*ly* to the adjectives from the word bank to make adverbs. Use the adverbs to complete the sentences below.**

curious   strong   loud   plain   generous

1. Our neighbor _____ offered to care for our cat while we were away.

2. I looked _____ inside the box, wondering what I'd find.

3. Danton dresses _____, but he always wears a bright orange hat.

4. Shania yelled _____ when she stubbed her toe.

5. My friends like soccer, but they _____ prefer basketball.

Name _____

Text and Graphic Features

Authors of informational text use **text features**, such as labels and headings, to further explain the information in the text. They use **graphic features**, such as illustrations and diagrams, to help explain ideas in the text.

> **Answer the questions about pages 78–79 of** *T.J. The Siberian Tiger Cub.*

1. What are the three types of graphic features on these pages?

_____

2. What information does each graphic feature give you?

_____

_____

3. How does the graph help readers understand the problem described in paragraph 9?

_____

_____

> **Answer the questions about page 80 of** *T.J. The Siberian Tiger Cub.*

4. What does the photograph show?

_____

5. What text feature helps you know what the photograph is showing?

_____

6. What information in the text does the photo help you better understand?

_____

Name _____

Words with /âr/ and /îr/

>> Read each sentence. Choose a word with /âr/ or /îr/ from the word bank that makes sense in the sentence. Write it in the blank. Reread the complete sentence to make sure it makes sense.

prepared	wherever	airline	careful
disappeared	clearly	peering	dairy

1. The _____ has ten airplanes.

2. Milk comes from cows who live on a _____ farm.

3. Grandma _____ a meal for the whole family.

4. We couldn't see the sun when it _____ behind some clouds.

5. The toddler follows his big brother _____ he goes.

6. We found Olivia _____ into the pond, looking for fish.

7. Be _____ with that knife when you cut the tomato.

8. The rules _____ say that there is no walking on the grass.

Central Idea

The **central idea** is what a text is mostly about. Clues, such as headings and visuals, help readers identify the central idea. Facts and other details provide evidence to support the central idea.

▶ **Answer the questions about page 84 of** *T.J. The Siberian Tiger Cub.*

1. What is the central idea in paragraphs 20 and 21?

_____

_____

_____

_____

2. How do the photo and caption support this idea?

_____

_____

_____

_____

3. What details in paragraph 21 support the idea that T.J. was having a wonderful time?

_____

_____

_____

_____

Name _____

Compound Words and Abbreviations

> Read each sentence. Find and underline the compound word. Draw a vertical line between the two smaller words that make up the compound word.

1. The park is only open in the daytime.

2. It was hard to ride my bike uphill.

3. After the storm, a big rainbow appeared in the sky.

4. Mikayla got new software for her computer.

5. We knew the baby was asleep because his eyelids were closed.

> Read each sentence. Find the abbreviation and underline the word it stands for.

6. Uncle Chris and Aunt Tanya live on Jefferson Ave.

        street   avenue   road

7. I had an appointment with Dr. Bridges yesterday.

        doctor   mister   nurse

8. Mr. Yang helped at the soup kitchen every weekend.

        doctor   mister   missus

Name _____

Critical Vocabulary

▶ Read each sentence. Decide which sentence best fits the meaning of the word in bold print. Circle the letter next to that sentence.

1. pollution

   a. The water in this stream is freezing cold in the spring.

   b. The water in this stream is so dirty that it is not safe to drink.

2. factories

   a. We took a tour of the buildings where boots and shoes are made.

   b. We went to the shopping center to look for new boots and shoes.

3. scarce

   a. Strawberries can be grown in many parts of the country.

   b. Strawberries grew wild here, but now only a few plants are left.

4. vertical

   a. Sarah climbed up the ladder to get to the top of the slide.

   b. Sarah kicked her feet harder as she raced across the pool.

5. greenhouses

   a. The farmer needs some new buildings where the chickens can live.

   b. The farmer used glass walls to build a place to grow lettuce and spinach.

6. crowded

   a. I bought some sweet, juicy peaches at the farmers' market.

   b. We tried to squeeze into the popular farmers' market.

7. vats

   a. Workers at the grove pick lemons that will be used for lemonade.

   b. The lemonade is mixed in huge tanks before it is put into bottles.

Name _____

Author's Purpose

An **author's purpose** is his or her reason for writing a text. The purpose may be to inform, to entertain, or to persuade. Knowing the purpose helps you understand the author's message.

▶ **Answer the questions about pages 106–107 of** *Farmer Will Allen and the Growing Table.*

1. What does the author want you to know about Will Allen?

_____

_____

2. Who is the author's intended audience for this biography?

_____

_____

Compound Words and Abbreviations

▶ **Read each sentence. Then choose a word from the word bank that completes the compound word in each sentence so that it makes sense. Write the word on the blank.**

news	bed	fighters	under

1. I _____ lined the title on the front page of my book report.

2. The _____ caster announced today's important events on television.

3. The orange chair in my _____ room is so comfortable.

4. Brave fire _____ responded to the alarm.

▶ **Read each sentence. Choose an abbreviation from the word bank that completes each sentence so that it makes sense. Write the word on the blank.**

Sr.	Mon.	Aug.	Blvd.

5. The first day of school is _____ 24th.

6. My dad, Jeremiah Green _____ , and I share the same name.

7. The park in our neighborhood is on Oak _____ .

8. Jose plays soccer on _____ and on Wed.

Name _____

Suffix –ion

A **suffix** is a word part added to the end of a base word that changes the meaning of the word.

The suffix –ion means "an act, result, or state of being." It changes a word into a noun. The base word's spelling changes slightly when adding –ion. For most words ending in e, the final e is dropped.

▸ **Write a noun to complete each sentence. Drop the e and add the suffix –ion to a base word from the word bank.**

    hesitate   create   collaborate   pollute   appreciate

1. The _____ between Lucy and Juan on the science project gave them the chance to share their best ideas.

2. Paul showed _____ before he stepped onto the stage.

3. The _____ in the water was harmful to the wildlife.

4. Dad's latest kitchen _____ contains every item from the refrigerator.

5. Jessie showed her _____ when she won the award.

Name _____

Text Structure

Text structure is the way information is organized in a text. One type of text structure is chronological. Another type is cause and effect.

> **Answer the questions about pages 102–105 of *Farmer Will Allen and the Growing Table*.**

1. How has the author organized the information in "The Kitchen Table"?

_____

2. What words and phrases are clues to the structure?

_____

3. Why has the author used this text structure in this section?

_____

_____

> **Answer the questions about page 109 of *Farmer Will Allen and the Growing Table*.**

4. How has the author organized the information in "Red Wiggler Worms"?

_____

5. How do you know?

_____

_____

6. Why has the author used this text structure in this section?

_____

_____

Name _____

Point of View

Point of view is the answer to this question: *Who is telling the story?*

- A narrator who is part of the story uses words such as *I*, *me*, and *we*.
- A narrator who is outside of the story uses words such as *he*, *she*, and *they*.

▶ **Answer the questions about page 104 of *Farmer Will Allen and the Growing Table*.**

1. Who is the narrator?

_____

2. Does the author use first-person or third-person point of view? How do you know?

_____

Name _____

Irregular Plurals

▶ Read each sentence. Identify and circle the irregular plural noun.

1. Two **gooses/geese** ran across the baseball fields.

2. Mai had to get braces to straighten her **tooths/teeth**.

3. The **men/mans** rode bicycles.

4. Did you see those two **deer/deers** in the meadow?

5. Mom cut the plums into **halfs/halves**.

6. My **feet/foots** had blisters after the hike.

7. We donated six **loaves/loafes** of bread to the food pantry.

8. The horse's **hooves/hoofs** clip-clopped on the pavement.

9. The mother lion took care of her three **offsprings/offspring**.

10. The **sheep/sheepes** had their babies in the springtime.

Name _____

Critical Vocabulary

You can use the words you learn from reading as you talk and write.

▶ **Use details and ideas from *One Plastic Bag* to support your answers to the questions below.**

1. What do the goats find when they **forage** near the road?

_____

_____

2. How do Isatou and her friends make **recycled** purses?

_____

_____

3. When Isatou **confesses**, what does she do?

_____

_____

▶ **Write a sentence using two of the Critical Vocabulary words. Include clues to each word's meaning in your sentence.**

_____

_____

Text Structure

Text structure is the way information is organized in a text.

▶ **Answer the questions about pages 120–121 of** *One Plastic Bag*.

1. What happens on page 120? What does this cause Isatou to do?

_____

_____

2. What text structure does the author use on these pages?

_____

▶ **Answer the questions about pages 126–127 of** *One Plastic Bag*.

3. How has the author organized the information in this section?

_____

4. Why does the author use this text structure?

_____

_____

▶ **Answer the questions about pages 128–131 of** *One Plastic Bag*.

5. What does the plastic bag problem cause Isatou and her friends to do first?

_____

6. What does the plastic bag problem cause Isatou and her friends to do after that?

_____

Name _____

Irregular Plurals

▶ **Read each sentence. Read the singular noun in parentheses. Write the plural form of the noun on the blank to complete the sentence.**

1. The _____ played together on a volleyball team. (woman)

2. Millions of _____ of insects live in the rain forest. (species)

3. I have several _____ growing on my windowsill. (cactus)

4. The park was crowded with lots of _____ on Saturday. (person)

5. Two _____ played on the swings. (child)

6. Jenna likes to wear her three favorite _____ during the winter. (scarf)

7. Two _____ pulled a cart. (ox)

8. We took three _____ last week. (quiz)

9. What is your favorite book _____ ? (series)

10. Many _____ take off and land in the airport each day. (aircraft)

Name _____

Critical Vocabulary

You can use the words you learn from reading as you talk and write.

> **Use details and ideas from *Energy Island* to support your answers to the questions below.**

1. What are some **renewable resources** the students think they could try to power the island?

_____

_____

2. What happened to make the people on Samsø **willing** to try new forms of energy?

_____

_____

3. How has the use of the undersea **cable** between Samsø and the mainland changed?

_____

_____

4. What makes Samsø an **environmental** leader for the rest of the world?

_____

_____

5. Why is it helpful when sunlight is **converted** to solar power?

_____

_____

Name _____

Point of View

Point of view is the answer to this question: *Who is telling the story?*

- A narrator who is part of the story uses words such as *I*, *me*, and *we*.
- A narrator who is outside of the story uses words such as *he*, *she*, and *they*.

Perspective is someone's attitude or feelings toward something.

▸ **Answer the questions about page 142 of *Energy Island*.**

1. Who is the narrator of this story?

_____

_____

2. What words are clues to who the narrator is? Is this first- or third-person point of view? Why?

_____

_____

_____

▸ **Answer the questions about pages 148–149 of *Energy Island*.**

3. How do the kids in Søren Hermansen's class feel about changing to renewable energy on Samsø?

_____

_____

Name _____

4. How is the adults' perspective different from the kids'?

_____

_____

5. Which side do you agree with? What is your perspective about renewable energy on Samsø?

_____

_____

Name _____

Generative
Vocabulary

Suffixes –ness and –able

A **suffix** is a word part added to the end of a base word that changes the meaning of the word.

The suffix –*ness* changes a word into a noun. For base words that end in *y*, change the *y* to *i* before adding –*ness*.

The suffix –*able* changes a word into an adjective. For base words ending in *e*, the final *e* often is dropped before adding –*able*.

> Add the suffix –*ness* or –*able* to the words below to form a noun or adjective. Then choose the best words to finish the story below.

kind _____

love _____

aware _____

distract _____

willing _____

When Mei heard the good news, she hugged her mom and thanked her for her _____ . Mei did a little dance around the kitchen. The family was finally going to get a pet!

Mom said they could go to the shelter on Saturday. Before that, Mei still had a lot of schoolwork to do. She tried to concentrate but was

easily _____ . She kept imagining a _____ kitten or puppy she could snuggle with at night.

Unfortunately, Mei had no _____ that her brother wanted a pet SNAKE.

Text and Graphic Features

Nonfiction text often includes **text features** such as headings and sidebars. This type of text may also include **graphic features** such as diagrams, maps, or illustrations.

▶ **Answer the questions about pages 142–143 of** *Energy Island.*

1. What graphic features are shown on pages 142–143?

_____

_____

2. How do the graphic features help you understand the text?

_____

_____

▶ **Answer the questions about pages 146–147 of** *Energy Island.*

3. What are the text features in the illustrations? How do they contribute to the text?

_____

_____

4. How is the information in the sidebar different from the information in the story?

_____

_____

Name _____

> **Answer the questions about pages 154–155 of *Energy Island*.**

5. How does the information in the sidebar connect to the part of the story on page 154?

_____

_____

6. How do the pinwheel toys in the illustrations earlier in the story connect with the sidebar?

_____

_____

Name _____

Words with /o͝o/ and /o͞o/

▶ Read each sentence. Find the word with the /o͝o/ or /o͞o/ sound and underline the letters that stand for that sound. Then underline the sound the letters stand for.

1. Marisol looked for her homework in her backpack.

   /o͞o/ sound   /o͝o/ sound

2. A big full moon rose in the sky.

   /o͞o/ sound   /o͝o/ sound

3. The roses were covered in drops of dew in the morning.

   /o͞o/ sound   /o͝o/ sound

4. The leaves on the tree shook when the big truck rumbled by.

   /o͞o/ sound   /o͝o/ sound

5. The detective searched for clues to solve the case.

   /o͞o/ sound   /o͝o/ sound

6. Please get the broom to sweep up the mess.

   /o͞o/ sound   /o͝o/ sound

7. That tricky joke really fooled me!

   /o͞o/ sound   /o͝o/ sound

8. Is it true that a spider has eight eyes?

   /o͞o/ sound   /o͝o/ sound

9. Fish swam in the little brook that flowed through the field.

   /o͞o/ sound   /o͝o/ sound

10. A red bird flew past my window.

    /o͞o/ sound   /o͝o/ sound

Name _____

Critical Vocabulary

> Read each sentence. Decide which sentence best fits the meaning of the word in bold print. Circle the letter next to that sentence.

1. flickered

   a. She replaced the light bulb after it began blinking off and on.

   b. She replaced the light bulb because it was too bright for the room.

2. concluded

   a. The concert ended with everyone singing together.

   b. The concert included talented musicians from all over the world.

3. preparations

   a. Alana left the party before me because she had homework to do.

   b. Alana finished getting ready for the party just before the guests arrived.

4. slender

   a. The tree's thin branches break easily in the wind.

   b. The tree's thick trunk and branches are easy to climb.

5. chimed

   a. We all spoke up in support of the new playground plans.

   b. We took turns voting on the new playground plans.

6. gallant

   a. My neighbor helped save the kittens from a burning building.

   b. My neighbor made us laugh with her stories about clown college.

Name _____

Literary Elements

Literary elements are the pieces that make up a story.

- **Characters** are the people and animals in a story.
- The **setting** is where and when the story takes place.
- **Events** are the things that happen in a story.

> **Answer the questions about pages 164–165 of *The Storyteller's Candle*.**

1. How does the author reveal the setting?

_____

_____

2. Who are the main characters?

_____

_____

3. How do you think the characters feel about living in New York?

_____

_____

> **Answer the following questions about page 175 of *The Storyteller's Candle*.**

4. Which character has made a big difference in the lives of Hildamar and Santiago's family and neighbors?

_____

_____

Name _____

5. How has Pura Belpré influenced what happens in the story?

_____

_____

_____

6. How are the children's and their neighbors' feelings different now than they were at the beginning of the story?

_____

_____

_____

Name _____

Compound Words

A **compound word** is a word made up of two smaller words. Look at the two smaller words to help you understand the meaning of the compound word.

▶ **Put together a word from the left column and a word from the right column to make a compound word that completes each sentence.**

under	plane
water	storm
rain	grown
over	fall
sleep	ground
air	over

1. Our canoe nearly went down a huge, roaring _____ .

2. I brought an umbrella just in case there is a _____ today.

3. During Kenan's _____ party, we stayed awake to watch a funny movie.

4. If you want to go to Europe, you need to take a boat or an

_____ .

5. Many animals burrow _____ to stay safe and warm.

6. The grass is so _____ that we can't find our kickball.

Name _____

Text and Graphic Features

Text features are kinds of type that are used for emphasis, such as color, bold text, or italic text.

Graphic features such as illustrations help explain ideas in the text. Illustrations show a scene from a story.

> **Answer the questions about pages 172–173 of *The Storyteller's Candle*.**

1. What story details does the illustration help you understand?

_____

_____

2. What details does the illustration include that are not in the text?

_____

_____

_____

_____

3. What moment in the story does the illustration show?

_____

_____

Words with /o͝o/ and /o͞o/

> Read each sentence. Choose a word from the word bank that contains the vowel sound shown below the blank that makes sense in the sentence. Write it in the blank.

/o͝o/ Sound	/o͞o/ Sound
crooked	cartoon
handbook	spewing
goodbye	classroom
fishhook	avenue

1. There are 20 students in our _____ .
/o͞o/ sound

2. Be careful because the _____ is sharp.
/o͝o/ sound

3. Nikko rode his bike along the _____ to school.
/o͞o/ sound

4. The Explorer's Club has a _____ that lists all the club rules.
/o͝o/ sound

5. The big factory was _____ smoke into the sky.
/o͞o/ sound

6. I love to watch funny _____ shows.
/o͞o/ sound

7. Someone needs to fix that _____ fence so that it is straight.
/o͝o/ sound

8. Mia waved _____ to her friend.
/o͝o/ sound

Figurative Language

Figurative language helps readers imagine the author's ideas or creates a special effect. **Similes** compare two different things using the word *like* or *as*. **Imagery** is language that describes how something looks, sounds, feels, smells, or tastes.

▶ **Answer the questions about page 169 of *The Storyteller's Candle*.**

1. What are the two similes in paragraph 17?

_____

_____

2. Which word signals that these are similes?

_____

3. In your own words, describe what the similes actually mean.

_____

_____

_____

_____

4. Which sensory word helps support the image that the storyteller's eyes are like *luceros*, or stars?

_____

_____

5. What sense can you use to imagine how something sparkled?

_____

Name _____

Review of Prefixes and Suffixes

▶ Read each sentence. Look at the word that is missing a prefix or suffix. Read the prefixes or suffixes under the sentence. Underline the prefix or suffix that completes the word. Write it on the line.

1. Julie can run fast_____ than me.

   er   est

2. Do you like hik_____ in the mountains?

   ed   ing

3. My family was _____pressed by my singing.

   im   non

4. Little Lily rode her red _____cycle.

   tri   mis

5. Please _____read the directions before making the soup.

   dis   pre

6. Asher went _____side to play board games.

   in   im

7. Is the sloth the slow_____ animal of all?

   er   est

8. She add_____ milk to her cereal.

   ed   ing

9. I don't eat eggplant because I _____like it.

   dis   mis

10. Is that old sailboat still sail_____ ?

    er   able

Name _____

Critical Vocabulary

You can use the words you learn from reading as you talk and write.

1 **Use what you learned about the vocabulary words from *Timeless Thomas*** **to help you finish each sentence.**

1. I think Edison's most **valuable** invention is _____ .

2. I had a **breakthrough** at school when _____ .

3. A **device** that would be hard to live without is _____ .

4. A good use of **technology** is _____ .

5. I would use **radar** to track _____ .

6. **Dictation** machines would be useful for _____ .

2 **Choose two of the Critical Vocabulary words and use them in a sentence.** **Include clues to each word's meaning in your sentence.**

_____

_____

Name _____

Text Structure

Text structure is the way information is organized in a text. An author uses a specific text structure to present information in a certain way. Examples of text structures include compare and contrast, cause and effect, chronology, and problem and solution.

> **Answer the questions about pages 210–211 of *Timeless Thomas: How Thomas Edison Changed Our Lives.***

1. What text structure has the author used on pages 210–211?

_____

_____

2. Which words in paragraph 27 are clues to this text structure?

_____

_____

3. Why does the author use this text structure on this and other pages in the text?

_____

_____

_____

_____

_____

Name _____

Review of Prefixes and Suffixes

Read the words in the word bank. Then read each sentence. Find a word from the word bank that completes the sentence. Write the word in the blank. Then read the sentence.

impressive	misspoke	paving	wasted
petted	inviting	hotter	prevented

1. Are you _____ Mara to your birthday party?

2. The leaky hose _____ a lot of water.

3. I gently _____ the horse on its head.

4. Workers were _____ the school parking lot with new blacktop.

5. I _____ when I told you the wrong time for the movie.

6. Jasper's seatbelt _____ him from getting hurt in the car crash.

7. The dancer is so _____ when she leaps and spins in the air!

8. The weather is much _____ today than it was yesterday.

Name _____

Greek Root graph and Suffix –logy

A **root** is a basic word part, usually from Greek or Latin, that carries meaning.
A **suffix** is a word part added to the end of a base word that changes the
meaning of the word.

> **Choose a word with the root *graph* or the suffix *–logy* to finish each sentence.**

volcanology   geographer   archaeology   autobiography
neurology   choreographer

1. Martina is a _____ . She studies Earth's geographical features
   and records detailed maps.

2. At the hospital we talked to a neurologist, or a doctor who studies the

   body's nervous system. He told us a lot about _____ .

3. The explorer was going to let a biographer write her life story, but then she

   decided to write the book herself. Her book will be an _____ .

4. Our talented _____ , Jon, taught us several new dances
   today. The show's choreography is going to be great!

5. If you want to make a career of studying volcanos, you can major in

   _____ in college.

6. Archaeologists have discovered many important clues to the past. A lot of
   what we know about ancient people is due to those who work in the field

   of _____ .

Name _____

Central Idea

The **central idea** of a text is what the text is mostly about. You can find the central idea of the whole text or of a section of the text. Authors include **supporting evidence**, or relevant **details**, that tell more about or support the central idea.

▶ Answer the questions about page 201 of *Timeless Thomas: How Thomas Edison Changed Our Lives.*

1. Which sentence states the central idea of the text on page 201?

_____

_____

_____

2. How do the illustrations support the text details in paragraph 8?

_____

_____

_____

▶ Choose another section of *Timeless Thomas: How Thomas Edison Changed Our Lives.*

3. What is the central idea of the section?

_____

4. What details support the central idea?

_____

Name _____

Text and Graphic Features

Informational text often includes **text features** such as headings, captions, and boldfaced words. Informational text also usually includes **graphic features**, such as photographs, illustrations, diagrams, and timelines.

▶ **Answer the questions about page 199 of** *Timeless Thomas: How Thomas Edison Changed Our Lives.*

1. What graphic features are on this page?

_____

_____

2. What does the diagram help you understand?

_____

_____

3. What text features support the diagram?

_____

▶ **Answer the questions about page 216 of** *Timeless Thomas: How Thomas Edison Changed Our Lives.*

4. What does the timeline show?

_____

5. What text and graphic features does the author use in the timeline?

_____

6. What does the timeline help readers understand?

_____

Prefixes re-, un- and Suffixes –less, –ness

Read each sentence. Choose the missing word from the word bank. Write the word. Then reread the completed sentence.

Name _____

swiftness	sleepless	rebuilt	tireless	happiness
unpacked	reminded	sadness	reheated	unsteadily

1. My puppy wags his tail and jumps on me to show his _____.

2. After it fell down, Sam _____ his tower of blocks.

3. The _____ dancer leaped gracefully across the stage.

4. Paul walked _____ across the swaying bridge.

5. Dad _____ our dinner when we came home late.

6. Our teacher _____ us that our report was due tomorrow.

7. The loud noises caused me to have a _____ night.

8. We packed and then _____ our suitcases after the trip.

9. The _____ of the runner helped her win the blue ribbon.

10. The lamb bleated with _____ until it spotted its mother.

Name _____

Critical Vocabulary

You can use the words you learn from reading as you talk and write.

▸ **Create a word web for each of the Critical Vocabulary words. In the center circle, write a Critical Vocabulary word. Then write words and phrases that are related to the Critical Vocabulary word in the outer circle. Discuss your word webs with a partner.**

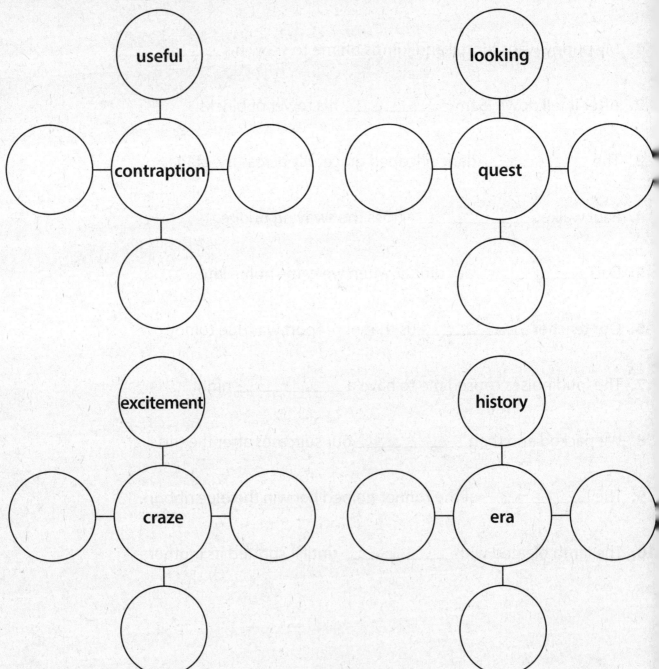

Name _____

Author's Purpose

The **author's purpose** is his or her reason for writing a text. Authors may write to inform, entertain, or persuade the reader.

▶ **Answer the questions about pages 222–223 of *The Bumpy Ride*.**

1. What is the author's purpose for writing this text?

_____

_____

_____

_____

2. How does the timeline develop the author's purpose?

_____

_____

_____

_____

Name _____

Prefixes *re-*, *un-* and Suffixes *–less*, *–ness*

▶ Read each sentence and the base word below it. Choose the correct prefix or suffix to add to the base word. Write the word. Then reread the completed sentence.

| re | un | less | ness |

1. Have you _____ your library book that was due?
   turned

2. A visit to the dentist was _____ for Nancy.
   pain

3. Do you enjoy the _____ of the summer rain?
   gentle

4. Dad _____ the living room wall.
   painted

5. Sue couldn't wait to _____ her birthday gift.
   wrap

6. Did you _____ that interesting story?
   read

7. Lions and tigers are not _____ .
   harm

8. If I have a _____ night, I am grouchy the next day.
   sleep

9. Mom wrapped our lunch, and then we _____ and ate it.
   wrapped

10. I enjoyed watching the _____ of the monkeys at the zoo.
    playful

Name _____

Critical Vocabulary

> Use the word line to answer each question. Then write an explanation for your answer.

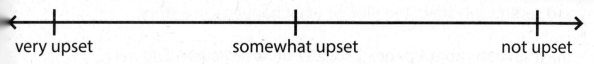

very upset   somewhat upset   not upset

How upset would you be if . . .

1. your school hired a **dynamo** to teach gym class?

_____

_____

2. the leaves you spent hours raking **whirled** away?

_____

_____

3. you were **perplexed** by a math problem?

_____

_____

4. an **engineer** built a time machine so you could go back or ahead in time?

_____

_____

5. judges at the science fair were **baffled** by your science project?

_____

_____

6. a skunk **lingered** at your house all day?

_____

_____

Literary Elements

Literary elements are the pieces that make up a story: characters, setting, plot, and events. Stories often have major and minor characters. Both the characters and setting can affect the plot, or what happens, in a story.

> **Answer the questions about pages 236–237 of *Rosie Revere, Engineer.***

1. Who are the major and minor characters on these pages? How do you know?

_____

_____

_____

2. Look at the illustration. How is Rosie different from her classmates?

_____

3. How does the attic setting influence Rosie's actions?

_____

> **Answer the questions about pages 240–241 of *Rosie Revere, Engineer.***

4. What do readers learn about a minor character on page 240?

_____

_____

5. How does the arrival of Great-Great Aunt Rose change the plot of the story?

_____

_____

Name _____ _____

Prefix ex–

A **prefix** is a word part added to the beginning of a base word that changes the meaning of the word.

▷ **Add the prefix _ex–_ to the words in the word bank to finish the sentences below.**

friends   dancer   doctor   neighbors   mayor

1. Jerome and Zev used to be buddies, but now they are _____ .

2. After we moved away, the people who used to live next door became

our _____ .

3. Devonte hurt his knee during a performance, so now he is an

_____ who is studying physics.

4. Ms. Rodriguez used to work at the hospital, but these days she is an

_____ and works on a goat farm.

5. In the movie, the _____ comes back to town and decides she
wants to run for office again.

Name _____

Figurative Language

Figurative language helps create a special effect or feeling in a story. **Imagery** is a type of figurative language that appeals to the readers' senses. Authors use imagery to engage readers and create images in their minds.

▶ **Answer the questions about page 241 of *Rosie Revere, Engineer.***

1. What type of figurative language is used in stanzas 9 and 10? How do you know?

_____

_____

_____

_____

2. Why has the author included these examples of personification?

_____

_____

_____

3. What image does the author use to describe the dawn? Why?

_____

_____

_____

_____

Plurals

▶ **Read each sentence. Identify and circle the correct singular or plural noun.**

1. Two **puppy/puppies** jumped and played in the yard.

2. We need to eat healthy food to keep our **body/bodies** strong.

3. Our school lunchroom buys fresh milk from a local **dairy/dairies**.

4. Dave and I went to the market to buy **grocery/groceries**.

5. Farms are not found in large **city/cities**.

6. Each student wrote a **story/stories** for our class book.

7. The **bunny/bunnies** were as soft as cotton.

8. I want to knit **booty/booties** for the new baby.

9. Have you ever ridden a **pony/ponies**?

10. Farm animals usually have their **baby/babies** in the springtime.

Name _____

Critical Vocabulary

▶ Use details and ideas from *Edison's Best Invention* to support your answers to the questions below.

1. What **system** was needed to make light bulbs work in New York City?

_____

_____

2. How did Edison's phonograph make **singles** possible?

_____

_____

3. What made Edison's power grid **innovative**?

_____

_____

4. What does the **compact** disc's name tell about how it stores information?

_____

_____

5. Why doesn't a **visionary** copy others' ideas?

_____

_____

6. What was **memorable** about how the country honored Edison when he died?

_____

_____

Identify Claim

In an opinion text, the author states a **claim** about a topic. The claim is the author's position or opinion on the topic. The author will present evidence to support the claim. The author thinks about the audience, or who will read the text, when determining what evidence to include.

▶ **Answer the questions about page 253 of** *Edison's Best Invention.*

1. What is the author's claim about the light bulb?

_____

_____

_____

2. Reread paragraph 3. Who is the author trying to persuade?

_____

_____

_____

_____

3. How does the author plan to persuade this audience?

_____

_____

_____

_____

Name _____

Latin Roots *vis* and *mem*

A **root** is a basic word part, usually from Greek or Latin, that carries meaning.

▶ **Choose a word with the root *vis* or *mem* to finish each sentence.**

memory   visibility   memorabilia   visual   memo   revisit

1. _____ is low on a foggy day like today. We can't even see the house next door!

2. I wrote a _____ to myself so I wouldn't forget to return the library books.

3. If you have a bad _____ for names, think of little tricks to help you, such as, "This person is great. Her name is Kate!"

4. A _____ artist is someone who draws, paints, or creates other kinds of art for people to look at.

5. Dani collects every kind of softball _____, from old balls to T-shirts.

6. When we _____ the beach, maybe we'll find some shells we missed the first time.

Name _____

Ideas and Support

Authors share their **ideas**, or opinions, and **support** them with facts and details. Opinions are beliefs and cannot be proven. Facts are statements that can be proven.

▶ **Answer the questions about page 257 of *Edison's Best Invention*.**

1. What support does the author give for claiming that the light bulb was Edison's best invention?

_____

_____

_____

_____

_____

2. Reread the last two sentences in paragraph 11. Do both statements seem factual? Explain.

_____

_____

_____

_____

Name _____

Plurals

> Read each sentence. Read the plural word in parentheses. Write the singular root word for the plural in the blank to complete the sentence.

1. Our _____ celebrated my grandpa's birthday. (families)

2. We invited our relatives and friends to his surprise _____ . (parties)

3. Grandpa will be _____ years old. (sixties)

4. Each person added Grandpa's favorite flower, a _____, to a special vase. (lilies)

5. A man and a _____ played their violins when he entered the room. (ladies)

6. Grandpa was so surprised that he began to _____ . (cries)

7. He was so happy to see his family and his best _____ . (buddies)

8. One friend arrived from a faraway _____ . (countries)

9. After dinner, we had cake and a special _____ . (pastries)

10. Each guest received a _____ of the group photo that was taken. (copies)

Name _____

Text and Graphic Features

Text and graphic features organize information in ways that help readers understand the ideas in a text. **Text features** include headings and captions. **Graphic features** include pictures and charts.

▶ **Answer the questions about page 262 of** *Edison's Best Invention.*

1. How is the chart organized?

_____

_____

2. What do the headings tell about?

_____

_____

3. What information is in the rows?

_____

_____

_____

4. Why did the author include this chart?

_____

_____

_____

Suffixes -ful, -y, -ly, -er, -or

> **Read each sentence. Choose the missing word from the word bank. Write the word. Then reread the completed sentence.**

runner	spoonful	closely	tailor	messy
windy	baker	graceful	bravely	conductor

1. On a _____ day, I have to hold on to my hat!

2. The first _____ of soup is the hottest.

3. The _____ dancer leaped across the stage.

4. Damian _____ walked across the swinging bridge.

5. That _____ makes the best muffins in town.

6. My _____ dog tracked mud across the floor.

7. The _____ collects tickets on the train.

8. If you need to have your pants shortened, you can take them to a _____ .

9. When the _____ crossed the finish line, she held her hands over her head in celebration.

10. The lamb followed _____ behind its mother so it wouldn't get lost.

Name _____

Critical Vocabulary

You can use the words you learn from reading as you talk and write.

▷ **Use what you learned about the vocabulary words from** *How Did That Get in My Lunchbox?* **to help you finish each sentence.**

1. Workers at the **dairy** are making _____ .

2. A food that can be **scarlet** is _____ .

3. Pickers in the **grove** fill their baskets with _____ .

4. Curds are pressed into _____ .

5. My tongue often feels **tingly** when _____ .

6. The farmer will cut down each **stalk** of _____ .

▷ **Choose two of the Critical Vocabulary words and use them in a sentence. Include clues to each word's meaning in your sentence.**

_____

_____

Name _____

Text Structure

Text structure is the way information is organized in a text. Authors choose a text structure that fits their purpose for writing. Examples of text structures include compare and contrast, cause and effect, sequence, and problem and solution.

▶ **Answer the questions about page 280 of** *How Did That Get in My Lunchbox?*

1. What are two ways that the author organizes the text on this page?

_____

2. What is the cause and its effect in paragraph 4? Use the word *because* in your answer.

_____

_____

▶ **Answer the questions about pages 286–287 of** *How Did That Get in My Lunchbox?*

3. What is the main text structure of paragraphs 18–22?

_____

4. Why does the author use that structure?

_____

5. What cause-effect connections does the author point out in steps 3 and 4? Why?

_____

_____

_____

Name _____

Suffixes –ful, –y, –ly, –er, –or

▷ **Read each sentence and the base word below it. Choose the correct suffix to add to the base word. Write the word. Then reread the completed sentence.**

ful	y	ly	er	or

1. The _____ ordered a snow day before the blizzard arrived.
   govern

2. Nancy needed to see a dentist about her _____ tooth.
   pain

3. The _____ knows the right time to plant each kind of flower.
   garden

4. Stan _____ is a fine artist.
   certain

5. Is it _____ to display a sports trophy?
   boast

6. The car swerved _____ to avoid the squirrel.
   sharp

7. Most frogs lay their eggs in a _____ location.
   water

8. If you don't get enough sleep, you might feel _____ .
   grouch

9. My friend is such a good _____ . I could talk to her all day.
   listen

10. The camp _____ made sure each camper had water for the hike.
    counsel

Name _____

Prefixes *in-* and *re-*; Suffix *-ful*

A **prefix** is a word part added to the beginning of a base word that changes the meaning of the word. A **suffix** is a word part added to the end of a base word that changes the meaning of the word.

▶ Add *in-*, *re-*, or *-ful* to a base word from the word bank to finish each sentence.

> pain   ability   fill   correct   beauty   adjust

1. Look at the _____ butterfly on that flower!

2. Will you please _____ Fifi's bowl with dog food?

3. I think this answer is _____, so I'll erase it and try again.

4. Mario needs to _____ his eyeglasses because they're still not straight.

5. My _____ to sing in tune means I probably won't join the chorus.

6. I dropped a piano on my toe, and that was quite _____ .

Name _____

Text and Graphic Features

Informational text often includes **text features,** such as headings, captions, and boldfaced words. Informational text also usually includes **graphic features**, such as photographs and diagrams.

▶ **Answer the questions about pages 280–281 of** *How Did That Get in My Lunchbox?*

1. How does the heading help readers?

_____

_____

_____

2. Why did the author include the diagram?

_____

_____

3. How are the labels and arrows helpful?

_____

_____

_____

Name _____

Central Idea

The **central idea** of a text is what the text is mostly about. Authors include **supporting evidence**, or relevant details, that tell more about the central idea.

> **Answer the questions about pages 278–279 of *How Did That Get in My Lunchbox?***

1. What question will this whole text answer?

_____

2. What is the central idea for the text?

_____

_____

> **Answer the questions about pages 282–283 of *How Did That Get in My Lunchbox?***

3. How does the detail about rennet support the central idea?

_____

4. How does the central idea on these pages support the central idea of the whole selection?

_____

> **Answer the question about page 292 of *How Did That Get in My Lunchbox?***

5. How does paragraph 34 help you understand the central idea of the text?

_____

_____

Name _____

Words with ough, augh

> Read each word in the first column. Say the vowel sound. Then in the second column, write two words from the word bank that have the same vowel sound.

plough	though	rough	fought	trough
bough	taught	cough	dough	tough

1. snow	
2. lawn	
3. cow	
4. stuff	
5. off	

Critical Vocabulary

You can use the words you learn from reading as you talk and write.

▶ **Use details and ideas from the video to support your answers to the questions below.**

1. Why is the **rotation** of crops good for the soil?

_____

_____

2. How is **prepping** helpful when cooking a meal?

_____

_____

3. What is something that you might keep in **storage**?

_____

_____

▶ **Choose two of the Critical Vocabulary words and use them in a sentence. Include clues to each word's meaning in your sentence.**

_____

_____

198

Name _____

Media Techniques

Video makers use **media techniques** to present information in different ways. Some examples of media techniques are sound effects, graphics, live action, and animation.

▶ **Answer the questions about the video** *Carrots, Farm to Fork.*

1. Why does the video include lots of shots of children in gardens and at markets?

_____

_____

2. What sound techniques did the video makers use to help viewers understand and enjoy the video?

_____

_____

_____

3. Why is Matthew Martin in this video?

_____

_____

_____

Name _____

Words with *ough, augh*

> Read each sentence. Choose the missing word from the word bank. Write the word. Then reread the completed sentence.

> | breakthrough | daughters | thoughtfulness |
> | although | roughly | retaught |
> | afterthought | laughter | sourdough |

1. Tammy will bake _____ bread to go with the vegetable soup.

2. Grace burst into _____ when she heard the funny story.

3. Bruce was grateful for his neighbor's _____ in picking up his mail.

4. Kofi only invited his cousin to the party as an _____ .

5. The doctor's discovery is a _____ in treating the illness.

6. Hector's car still runs well, _____ it is old.

7. The teacher _____ the math concept the students didn't understand.

8. That town is _____ ten miles from here.

9. The woman took her twin _____ to the movies.

Name _____

Critical Vocabulary

You can use the words you learn from reading as you talk and write.

▷ **Use details and ideas from** *How Do You Raise a Raisin?* **to support your answers to the questions below.**

1. What causes grapes to **shrivel**?

_____

_____

2. When might it be helpful to have a **burly** friend?

_____

_____

3. What is something that grows on a **vine**?

_____

_____

▷ **Write a sentence using two of the Critical Vocabulary words. Include clues to each word's meaning in your sentence.**

_____

_____

Figurative Language

Figurative language is language that has a special meaning that is different from its dictionary definition. **Imagery** is language that appeals to readers' senses. Authors use **similes** to compare things using the word *like* or *as*.

▶ **Answer the questions about page 305 of *How Do You Raise a Raisin?***

1. What image do the names "Raisinfield" and "Raisinville" help create?

_____

2. How is this figurative language different from the facts about where raisins grow?

_____

_____

3. Why does the author use the word "cuttings" in quotation marks?

_____

▶ **Answer the questions about pages 306–307 of *How Do You Raise a Raisin?***

4. What image do the phrases "sprawling branches" and "tamer train them" create? Why?

_____

_____

5. What simile is used in paragraph 19?

_____

6. Why does the author use this simile?

_____

Name _____

Suffixes –ness and –able

A **suffix** is a word part added to the end of a base word that changes the meaning of the word.

> **Add the suffix *–ness* or *–able* to the words below to form a noun or adjective. Then choose the best words to finish the sentences below.**

bold: _____

believe: _____

fix: _____

delicious: _____

debate: _____

I admire the bunny's bravery and _____ in the

story, but the plot is not very _____ . Would a

rabbit really be so bold when facing a hungry tiger? You know that tiger must

be imagining the _____ of a rabbit dinner. If the

rabbit got close to the tiger, that big cat would bite off at least one of the

bunny's legs. Then those legs would be gone for good, and the bunny would

have a problem that is not _____ . Honestly,

it's not even _____ whether the bunny is being

smart or foolish in this story.

Text and Graphic Features

Informational text often includes **text features,** such as boldface or italic text, numbered lists, and sidebars. Informational text also usually includes **graphic features**, such as photographs or illustrations.

▶ **Answer the questions about page 304 of** *How Do You Raise a Raisin?*

1. What are the two main fonts, or typefaces, found on this page and throughout the text?

_____

_____

2. What are their purposes?

_____

_____

▶ **Answer the questions about page 309 of** *How Do You Raise a Raisin?*

3. Why did the illustrator include raisins acting like people?

_____

4. What does the numbered list show?

_____

_____

5. What fact does the illustration of the honeybees below paragraph 28 support?

_____

Name _____

Words with /j/ and /s/

Write the word from the word bank that best replaces the underlined word or words in each sentence.

nudge	icing	merge
cycle	twice	pudgy
piece	gem	racing

1. The two hiking paths join together by the river.   _____

2. The baby waved her plump little fingers at me.   _____

3. Would you like vanilla or chocolate frosting on the cake?   _____

4. Jonas is rushing to the library before it closes.   _____

5. The ruby in that ring is a priceless jewel.   _____

6. I went to the beach two times last summer.   _____

7. Kane gave the sled a little push to start it down the hill.   _____

8. Sara will ride a bike to the post office today.   _____

9. One part of this puzzle is missing!   _____

Critical Vocabulary

> Read each sentence. Decide which sentence best fits the meaning of the word in bold print. Circle the letter next to that sentence.

1. layout

   a. The other teachers thought Ms. McCarthy had a nice garden.

   b. The plan showed where each kind of vegetable would be planted.

2. mulch

   a. Some students spread straw on the ground to protect the plants.

   b. Some students took buckets of food scraps out to the compost pile.

3. arbor

   a. We walked through a tunnel made of tree branches.

   b. We walked through a garden near a forest of tall trees.

4. transplanted

   a. Plants grew in clay pots in the warm greenhouse.

   b. I moved a seedling from a pot in the greenhouse into a garden bed.

5. kernels

   a. She picked the small yellow seeds off the corncob.

   b. She picked several ears of corn off each cornstalk.

6. blooming

   a. The apples are ripe and ready to be picked.

   b. The apple tree is covered in pink flowers.

Name _____

Text Structure

Text structure is the way information is organized in a text. Authors use specific text structures to support their purpose for writing. Examples of text structures include compare and contrast, cause and effect, sequence, and problem and solution.

▶ **Answer the questions about page 327 of *It's Our Garden*.**

1. What is the structure of this part of the text?

_____

_____

2. How do you know?

_____

_____

_____

3. Why did the author choose this text structure?

_____

_____

_____

_____

Name _____

Suffix –ion and Compound Words

A **suffix** is a word part added to the end of a base word that changes its meaning and part of speech. A **compound word** is made up of two smaller words.

> **Add the suffix *–ion* to each verb in bold to complete each sentence.**

1. When I **graduate** from school, will you come to my _____ ?

2. If we **inflate** this tire all the way, it will reach its peak level

of _____ .

3. The heat is beginning to **radiate** through the room, and soon its

_____ will make us warm and toasty.

4. I **appreciate** all your help, so I got you a gift to show my _____ .

> **Put together a word from the left column and a word from the right column to make a compound word that completes each sentence.**

under	breaker
wind	look
thunder	water
over	storm

1. If we dive into the ocean here, we can reach the _____ cave.

2. During the _____, lightning bolts cracked through the sky.

3. Please put on your _____ because of the chilly breeze.

4. Don't _____ the recipe's details, or the bread will end up dry.

Name _____

Content-Area Words

Content-area words are words that are specific to an area of study, such as math, science, or social studies. Use **context clues**, or nearby words and sentences, to figure out the meaning of a content-area word.

> **Answer the questions about page 319 of *It's Our Garden*.**

1. How can you tell what *compost* means?

_____

_____

_____

_____

2. Why is it important to know the meaning of *compost* in a text about a garden?

_____

_____

_____

_____

Name _____

Words with /j/ and /s/

> Read each question and choose an answer from the word bank. Write the word.

> | apology | luggage | cyclone |
> | scissors | recess | bandage |
> | surface | certain | generous |

1. What can you use to cut paper? _____

2. What word describes a person who shares with others? _____

3. What could you use to cover a cut on your arm? _____

4. What is it you give when you say you're sorry? _____

5. What word names a strong windstorm? _____

6. Which word means almost the same as *sure*? _____

7. What might you pack for traveling? _____

8. What do you call a break at school? _____

9. What is the outer layer of something called? _____

Name _____

Point of View

Point of view describes how readers experience a story or text. Stories and texts can be told through a **first-person** point of view or a **third-person** point of view.

▶ **Answer the questions about page 317 of *It's Our Garden*.**

1. Is this text told with a first-person or a third-person narrator?

_____

_____

_____

2. How can you tell which point of view this story is told in?

_____

_____

_____

_____

Final Stable Syllables –tion, –sure, –ture

> Read each clue. Write a word from the word bank to answer each clue.

fiction	nation	vulture	station	puncture
unsure	future	portion	moisture	closure

1. There is lots of this in the air on a foggy day.   _____

2. This is part of a whole.   _____

3. This is a kind of made-up story.   _____

4. This means the shutting down of something.   _____

5. This is another word for *country*.   _____

6. A nail could do this to a bike tire.   _____

7. This large bird eats dead animals.   _____

8. This is a place to get on a bus.   _____

9. This means you are not really certain of something.   _____

10. This is the time yet to come.   _____

Name _____

Critical Vocabulary

▶ **Circle the letter of the sentence that fits the meaning of the word in bold.**

1. cinders

  a. We gathered small, dry sticks to help start a fire for our cookout.

  b. After our cookout, only blackened bits and chunks of coal were left.

2. belched

  a. Great puffs of black smoke blasted from the chimney.

  b. Smoke gently curled out of the chimney and into the sky.

3. barren

  a. As I looked across the desert, I saw nothing but sand.

  b. As I looked across the meadow, I saw blooming flowers.

4. lagoon

  a. Our canoe splashed down the tumbling river.

  b. I splashed happily in the quiet, blue waters.

5. garlands

  a. We were given bunches of colorful flowers to put in the vases.

  b. We were given rings of colorful flowers to wear around our necks.

6. appease

  a. When my little brother is hungry and cranky, I give him a snack.

  b. When my little brother yawns and gets sleepy, I sing a song to him.

Author's Craft

Author's craft is the language and techniques an author uses to make his or her writing interesting. Author's craft includes the author's voice and tone and the mood that is created.

> **Answer the questions about page 355 of _When the Giant Stirred._**

1. How is the author's voice like the voice of a storyteller?

_____

_____

_____

_____

_____

2. Which word best describes the author's tone—_joyful_ or _serious_? Why?

_____

_____

_____

3. How do the text and illustration create the mood and inspire the feelings that readers experience?

_____

_____

_____

_____

_____

Name _____

Final Stable Syllables –tion, –sure, –ture

> Read each sentence. Choose the missing word from the word bank. Write the word. Then reread the completed sentence.

selection	posture	leisurely
location	enclosure	motion
reassure	pollution	sculpture

1. Can you find our _____ on the map?

2. That _____ of a bear is very lifelike.

3. The café is a _____ walk from our hotel.

4. The donkeys are kept in an _____ on the ranch.

5. The stars are in constant _____ .

6. You can improve your _____ by standing up straight.

7. The corner market has a good _____ of fruit.

8. The doctor will _____ the patient that she will be well soon.

9. How can the city work to clean up air _____ ?

Name _____

Prefix re–, Suffix –y, Root graph

A **prefix** is a word part added to the beginning of a base word that changes the meaning of the word. A **suffix** is a word part added to the end of a base word that changes the meaning of the word. A **root** is a basic word part, usually from Greek or Latin, that carries meaning.

▶ Choose a word with the prefix *re–*, the suffix *–y*, or the root *graph* to finish each sentence.

> choosy   autograph   lazy   cheery   paragraph   replace

1. I asked the singer to sign my concert ticket, but instead she gave me a

photo with her _____ and a note!

2. My cat likes nothing better than lying in the sun all day and acting as

_____ as possible.

3. You probably should _____ those broken glasses with a new pair before you walk straight into a tree trunk.

4. Raffi is very _____ about his clothes and can spend an hour picking the perfect outfit.

5. Ms. Demarco told us to write at least one _____ explaining what we did last weekend.

6. Are you whistling because you feel _____ on this beautiful spring day, or are you just trying to annoy me?

Name _____

Theme

The **theme** is the main message, lesson, or moral of a text.

▶ **Answer the questions about page 366 of *When the Giant Stirred*.**

1. What is the theme of this legend?

_____

_____

_____

_____

_____

_____

2. What details throughout the plot help develop the theme?

_____

_____

_____

_____

_____

_____

Figurative Language

Figurative language can create a special effect or feeling in a text. Both imagery and alliteration create special effects. Figurative language also includes figures of speech that show comparison, such as similes.

▶ **Answer the questions about page 350 of *When the Giant Stirred*.**

1. What is the simile on this page?

_____

2. Is the mountain really a giant?

_____

3. Describe the effect of the author's use of this figurative language.

_____

_____

▶ **Answer the questions about page 363 of *When the Giant Stirred*.**

4. What type of figurative language is the phrase "in its fury"? Why might the author have chosen to use this phrase?

_____

_____

5. Reread paragraph 22. Why might the author have decided to use alliteration?

_____

_____

_____

VCCV Syllable Division Pattern

> Divide each word in the word bank into syllables. Write the word from the word bank to finish the second sentence in each pair.

window	attic	cursor	artist
thunder	dinner	factory	pencil

1. A storm can have lightning.

It can also have _____ .

2. You can draw with a crayon.

You can write with a _____ .

3. People in a store sell things.

People in a _____ make things.

4. You eat breakfast in the morning.

You eat _____ at night.

5. The basement is at the bottom of a house.

The _____ is at the top.

6. Keys are on a computer keyboard.

The _____ is a movable marker on the computer screen.

7. You walk through a door.

You look through a _____ .

8. An author writes books.

An _____ paints pictures.

Name _____

Critical Vocabulary

You can use the words you learn from reading as you talk and write.

▶ **Use the word line to answer each question. Then explain your answer.**

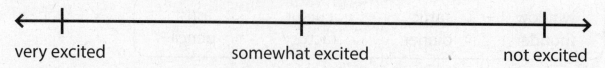

←————|————————————|————————————|————→

very excited   somewhat excited   not excited

How excited would you be if . . .

1. you could have a **tempting** dessert?

_____

_____

2. your dog started growling **ominously**?

_____

_____

3. you were asked to wash large **quantities** of dirty dishes?

_____

_____

▶ **Choose two of the Critical Vocabulary words and use them in a sentence. Include clues to each word's meaning in your sentence.**

_____

_____

Name _____

Theme

The **theme** is the message, lesson, or moral of a story.

> **Answer the questions about pages 373–376 of *Why the Sky Is Far Away*.**

1. How did the people get their food in the beginning of the tale?

_____

_____

2. Why did the sky warn King Oba?

_____

_____

_____

3. Did the sky's warning work? Explain.

_____

_____

_____

_____

_____

4. What is the theme of this folktale?

_____

_____

Name _____

VCCV Syllable Division Pattern

▶ **Read each sentence. Choose the missing word from the word bank. Write the word. Then reread the completed sentence.**

ribbon	chimney	sentence
remember	blister	insect
mascot	channel	collection

1. The ferry carries passengers across the _____ .

2. Do you _____ what time the meeting starts?

3. The smoke rose out of the _____ .

4. The team's _____ waved a banner!

5. Sandy won a blue _____ at the county fair.

6. A beetle is an _____ .

7. My brother has a big coin _____ .

8. Ruth got a _____ on her foot after the long hike.

9. Jed misspelled a word in his _____ .

Critical Vocabulary

You can use the words you learn from reading as you talk and write.

▷ **Use details and ideas from *Cinder Al and the Stinky Footwear* to help you finish each sentence.**

1. Princess Peeyu needed someone to dance with at the

upcoming _____ .

2. The princess issued a **proclamation** about _____ .

3. Cinder Al's brothers **snickered** because _____ .

4. Princess Peeyu's **pungent** shoes smelled like _____ .

▷ **Write a sentence using two of the Critical Vocabulary words. Include clues to each word's meaning in your sentence.**

_____

_____

Name _____

Author's Craft

Author's craft is the language an author uses to make his or her writing interesting and to communicate ideas to the reader.

▶ **Answer the questions about page 382 of *Cinder Al and the Stinky Footwear.***

1. How would you describe the author's voice and tone in this story?

_____

_____

_____

_____

2. Why might the author have decided to use hyperbole?

_____

_____

_____

_____

3. What words might best describe the mood, or the feelings that readers experience?

_____

_____

_____

_____

Name _____

Suffix –ment

A **suffix** is a word part added to the end of a base word that changes the meaning of the word.

▷ **Add the suffix –*ment* to each word below to form a noun. Then choose the best word to finish each sentence.**

merry: _____

disappoint: _____

adjust: _____

nourish: _____

enchant: _____

ship: _____

1. I haven't eaten all day and desperately need some _____!

2. Can you make an _____ to this jacket so it fits me better?

3. The story is set in a land of make-believe and _____ where everyone's wishes come true.

4. Marcos felt deep _____ when he learned his favorite brother would be away all summer.

5. Yesterday a boat brought a large _____ of supplies to the island's residents.

6. Elspeth's party was full of laughs and _____ .

Name _____

Figurative Language

Authors use **figurative language**, such as **imagery** and **alliteration**, to create a special effect or feeling in a text. Figurative language also includes figures of speech that show comparison, such as **similes**.

▶ **Answer the questions about page 384 of** *Cinder Al and the Stinky Footwear.*

1. What is compared in the simile in paragraph 6?

_____

_____

_____

2. Why did the author use this simile and others like it?

_____

_____

_____

3. What is the effect of alliteration on readers?

_____

_____

_____

_____

Name _____

Words Ending in –*le*, –*al*, –*el*, –*er*

> Read the words in the word bank. Then choose the word that best matches each clue.

saddle	member	nickel	triple	camel
supper	petal	cradle	better	royal

1. part of a flower _____

2. the opposite of *worse* _____

3. an animal found in the desert _____

4. someone who belongs to a group _____

5. to make three times greater _____

6. a bed for a baby _____

7. having to do with a king _____

8. a five-cent coin _____

9. a meal you eat late in the day _____

10. used to ride a horse _____

Name _____

Critical Vocabulary

You can use the words you learn from reading as you talk and write.

▶ **Use details and ideas from *Compay Mono and Comay Jicotea* to support your answers to the questions below.**

1. What are some reasons Compay Mono **inspected** his crops each day?

_____

2. What does Compay Mono do when he discovers the **theft** of his pumpkins?

_____

3. What does Comay Jicotea do to show she is **sympathetic**?

_____

4. What is **suspicious** about the way the crops were stolen?

_____

5. What text evidence shows that Compay Mono may be as **crafty** as Comay Jicotea?

_____

6. What **reputation** will Comay Jicotea have after what happens in the story?

_____

▶ **Choose two of the Critical Vocabulary words and use them in a sentence.**

_____

_____

Name _____

Author's Purpose

An **author's purpose** is his or her reason for writing. Authors may write to persuade, inform, or entertain readers.

▶ **Answer the questions about pages 392–394 of** *Compay Mono and Comay Jicotea.*

1. How do paragraphs 1–5 show the author's purpose?

_____

_____

_____

_____

_____

2. How does the author prepare readers for the problem in the story?

_____

_____

_____

_____

_____

_____

_____

Name _____

Prefixes *im-*, *in-*

A **prefix** is a word part added to the beginning of a base word that changes the meaning of the word.

> **Use a word from the word bank to finish each sentence below.**

| impolite | insincere | immature | indefinite | imbalance | indecisive |

1. There is an _____ in our teams, so one person should move to the other team.

2. Jeannie forgot to thank her grandfather and worried that she would

   seem _____ .

3. I'm feeling _____ and can't make up my mind about which movie to watch.

4. Is Troy being _____ when he says he wants to come to the amusement park? I know he doesn't like roller coasters.

5. Some people accuse me of being _____ because I still like to sleep with a teddy bear.

6. We're going to visit my aunt sometime next spring, but the date is

   still _____ .

Name _____

Literary Elements

Literary elements are the pieces that make up a story. The **characters** are the people or animals in a story. The **setting** is where and when a story takes place. The **plot** describes the conflict, or problem the characters face, and the resolution, or how the problem is solved.

> **Answer the questions about page 396 of *Compay Mono and Comay Jicotea.***

1. Who is the major character?

_____

_____

_____

_____

2. What role does the minor character play in the story?

_____

_____

_____

_____

3. How does the plot change in the new setting shown on pages 396–397?

_____

_____

_____

_____

Name _____

Words Ending *in –le, -al, -el, -er*

▶ **Write the word from the word bank that best replaces the underlined word or words in each sentence.**

```
┌─────────────────────────────────────────────────────┐
│    triangle        annual         shovel             │
│    quarrel         invisible      passenger          │
│    principal       another        mural              │
└─────────────────────────────────────────────────────┘
```

1. The taxi driver picked up a <u>rider</u>.   _____

2. My cousins had a <u>disagreement</u> about money.   _____

3. Doris drew a <u>three-sided shape</u> on her paper.   _____

4. The club holds their <u>yearly</u> meeting at the library.   _____

5. Phil would like <u>one more</u> apple.   _____

6. The air around us is <u>not able to be seen</u>.   _____

7. The artist created a <u>wall painting</u> at city hall.   _____

8. The gardener uses a <u>digging tool</u> when she plants trees.   _____

9. The <u>head of the school</u> made an announcement.   _____

Name _____

Theme

The **theme** is the message, lesson, or moral in a story.

▶ **Answer the questions about page 398 of** *Compay Mono and Comay Jicotea.*

1. What real-life observation is the topic of this page?

_____

_____

_____

2. What are the themes of this story?

_____

_____

_____

Name _____

Position-Based Spellings

▶ Read each sentence. Look at the word with missing letters. Choose the letters that correctly complete the word. Write them on the blank.

1. Have a seat on the blue c_____ch.

    ou   ow

2. Today, I wore two different socks that don't ma_____.

    ch   tch

3. The little pig said, "_____nk."

    oi   oy

4. The farmer will pl_____ the field before planting the corn.

    ou   ow

5. Would you like to mar_____ in the parade with the band?

    ch   tch

6. Is that your friend Tr_____ from class?

    oi   oy

7. His fr_____n showed that he was unhappy.

    ou   ow

8. May I have a snack after lun_____?

    ch   tch

9. The recipe says to b_____l the water.

    oi   oy

10. Ella gave a spee_____ about keeping our school clean.

    ch   tch

Position-Based Spellings

> Read each sentence. Choose a word from the box that makes sense in the sentence. Write it in the blank. Reread the complete sentence.

choices	wildflowers	marching	enjoys
breakdown	fetching	discount	allow

1. My dog is really good at _____ a ball.

2. Daniel really _____ playing outside on a nice day.

3. The store offers a _____, which makes its prices lower.

4. Yellow and orange _____ grew in the field.

5. Will your parents _____ you to stay up late on the weekend?

6. We saw the _____ band in the parade.

7. I can't decide because there are so many _____ !

8. The car with a flat tire rolled into the _____ lane.

Name _____

Words That Begin with a- or be-

> Read each sentence. Look at the word in bold print. Underline the syllable in which you hear the schwa sound.

1. The bee buzzed **above** our heads.

2. What just moved **behind** that tree?

3. May I come **along** with you to the park?

4. The kitten is hiding **between** the two chairs.

5. I'm going outside **because** the weather is so nice.

6. Does this jacket **belong** to anyone?

7. Our teacher read the story **aloud**.

8. I'm not **afraid** of the dark.

9. What's that movie **about**?

10. **Beware** of the slippery sidewalk.

Words That Begin with a- or be-

> Read each sentence. Choose a word from the box that makes sense in the sentence. Write it in the blank. Reread the complete sentence.

beginner	apologized	betrayed	ahead
agreement	bejeweled	another	behavior

1. I like to plan _____ for bad weather by always carrying an umbrella.

2. The royal crown was _____ with diamonds and rubies.

3. I'd like _____ piece of pizza, please.

4. Everyone in the _____ band is learning to play new instruments.

5. The teacher praised our class for good _____ .

6. Kaylee and I have an _____ that we will help each other study for the quiz.

7. I _____ to my brother for breaking his toy.

8. If you lie to me, I will feel that you have _____ me.

Open and Closed Syllables Review

▶ Read each sentence. Look at the word in bold print. Rewrite the word on the
line. Draw a line between the syllables in the word you wrote.

1. Please put the laundry in the **basket**.

   _____

2. Did you make **salad** for lunch?

   _____

3. The weather is so **humid** today.

   _____

4. Have you **spoken** to Lily lately?

   _____

5. I didn't **expect** it to be so cold today.

   _____

6. Our class is reading a new **novel**.

   _____

7. Will you hand me the **hammer** so I can fix this nail?

   _____

8. I like to **visit** my grandparents.

   _____

9. The teacher will be here in a **moment**.

   _____

10. Did you answer the **bonus** question on the quiz?

   _____

Name _____

Open and Closed Syllables Review

Read each sentence. Choose the missing word from the box. Write it in the blank. Then reread the complete sentence.

pavement	littering	tabletop
portions	chattering	lemonade
structure	finally	volleyball

1. The squirrel was _____ loudly up in the tree.

2. Jacob spilled milk all over the _____ .

3. Do you want to join our _____ team?

4. People should stop _____ in order to keep our parks clean.

5. I like to drink cool _____ on a hot day.

6. The restaurant serves very big _____ of food.

7. I scraped my knee on the _____ .

8. We built a huge _____ with blocks.

9. At last, I _____ beat Dad at checkers!

Self-Correction Strategy

▶ Read each question and choose an answer from the box. Write the word.

frozen	subtract	comic
legend	greeting	bacon
banner	vanish	cricket

1. What kind of story comes from the past? _____

2. What is the opposite of *add*? _____

3. What is another word for *disappear*? _____

4. Which word names a relative of a grasshopper? _____

5. What is another word for *flag*? _____

6. On what kind of pond can you ice skate? _____

7. What do you call words of welcome? _____

8. What might you eat with eggs and toast? _____

9. What kind of book can make you laugh? _____

Name _____

Self-Correction Strategy

> Read each sentence. Choose the missing word from the box. Write the word. Then reread the completed sentence.

cabinet	promise	shriveling
ambulance	natural	college
studio	microwave	labels

1. Quinn's sister studies Math at _____ .

2. The _____ is on its way to the hospital.

3. My friend made a _____ to visit me this summer.

4. Ned can reheat the leftovers in the _____ oven.

5. It's a good idea to read the _____ on food packages.

6. The artist paints in her _____ .

7. It is _____ for dolphins to swim.

8. The hot sun is _____ the tomato plants.

9. Please put the dishes in the _____ .

Related Words

> Read each sentence and look at the underlined word. Write a related word or words to help you think about its meaning.

1. Joan's shirt has a pattern of <u>horizontal</u> stripes.

   _____

2. Trey offered a reward for his <u>stolen</u> bike.

   _____

3. Nadia is <u>lonesome</u> without her friends around.

   _____

4. Dad's train arrives today at the <u>central</u> station in the city.

   _____

5. Ms. Jennings works as an <u>assistant</u> in the science lab.

   _____

6. Val needed <u>dental</u> work after her braces were removed.

   _____

7. Cyrus had perfect <u>attendance</u> for the school year.

   _____

Name _____

Related Words

▷ Read each word. Think of and write a related word or words. Then write a definition for the first word.

1. approval _____

_____

2. comparison _____

_____

3. circular _____

_____

4. transforming _____

_____

5. signature _____

_____

6. muscular _____

_____

Name _____

Words with Affixes

▶ Read each clue. Write a word from the box to answer each clue. Then circle the prefix or suffix in each word.

rebuild	unheard	shapeless	neatness	restart
happiness	restful	unclean	displeased	agreement

1. not free from dirt	_____
2. to begin again	_____
3. the act of having the same idea	_____
4. not feeling pleasure	_____
5. without a definite outline	_____
6. to construct again	_____
7. a state of being or feeling very glad	_____
8. full of peace and quiet	_____
9. not listened to	_____
10. being orderly	_____

Name _____

Words with Affixes

Read each sentence. Underline the word in each sentence that has a prefix or suffix. Circle the prefix or suffix in each word.

1. Joining a soccer team involves making a big time commitment.

2. Gina was surprised by the unplanned success of her singing career.

3. Students should always be respectful of their teachers.

4. The secret code appeared as a meaningless jumble of letters.

5. Larry likes to rearrange the furniture in his bedroom every so often.

6. The best friends were able to reunite after spending many years apart.

7. There are many unanswered questions about the universe.

8. The hawk swooped towards the ground with an effortless dive.

9. Tara's closet was so disorganized she couldn't find her raincoat.

10. The hospital patient felt a wave of dizziness when he stood up.